Praise for

REBRANDING THE CHURCH

"Dr. Eric Mason has never been afraid to tell the truth, even when it hurts. In *Rebranding the Church*, he doesn't just diagnose the problem; he calls us back to something deeper, older, and more powerful than image: identity. This isn't a book about aesthetics. It's a call for the people of God to embody the character of Christ again. If you're tired of seeing the church be known more for scandals than service, this book will shake you, ground you, and send you. It's biblical. It's bold. And it's exactly what we need right now."

—LECRAE, artist, author, and founder of Reach Records

"Dr. Eric Mason has produced an instant classic. This work is the challenging, inspiring, and insightful book that we need for our current times. He exposes the current crisis facing Christianity in America and gives us a game plan for how we can be a part of the solution. *Rebranding the Church* is required reading for Christians seeking to live as the witnesses God has called us to be as we navigate today's culture. Dr. Mason has given us the book we had all been desperately waiting for to call us to become a better expression of the church in this current season."

—BRYAN CARTER, senior pastor of Concord Church, Dallas

"A brand is the public perception of who you are and who you purport yourself to be. In *Rebranding the Church*, Dr. Eric Mason effectively unveils the need, challenges, and methods to reboot the church's brand so that it relevantly and accurately reflects what it was divinely created to be. This book will help and inspire the church to go to the next level in the spiritual development of its members and maximize its impact in the world."

—DR. TONY EVANS, president of The Urban Alternative
and founder of Oak Cliff Bible Fellowship

"Dr. Eric Mason continues trailblazing for the church. With his trademark combination of theological acumen, street savvy, and pastoral experience, his new book charts a fresh path forward for faithful ministry in the twenty-first century. While acknowledging the church's very real failures and flaws, Dr. Mason refuses to take the easy route of mere complaint and critique. Instead, he provides a positive and hopeful framework for pastors, leaders, and church members that is simultaneously practical, accessible, and robust."

—Dr. STEVE BEZNER, associate professor of pastoral ministry at George W. Truett Theological Seminary and author of *Your Jesus Is Too American*

"The church has a well-earned branding problem. Like a soul food restaurant that only sells kale salads, too many people find themselves coming to church for one thing, only to leave disappointed when they experience the opposite—tragic things. My friend Dr. Eric Mason not only helps center the church in the good news of the Bible but also does it in a way that when you finish this book, you will find yourself full of hope."

—DR. BRYAN LORITTS, author of *Grace to Overcome*

"*Rebranding the Church* captures the essence of what most Americans think about church and why and how the church can get back to its original 'branding' of gospel centrality, discipleship, service, and generosity. Dr. Mason brilliantly and pastorally equips readers with both biblical knowledge and practical tools to engage culture relevantly without indulging in the ideologies that will cause the church to drift from its primary mission. This book is essential reading for ministry leaders, their teams, and the body of Christ at large!"

—JEROME GAY, JR., pastor and author of *Church Hurt: Holding the Church Accountable and Helping Hurt People Heal*

"In an age of echoes, Dr. Eric Mason is a voice of clarity and truth. I am a firsthand witness and beneficiary of his ministry and friendship. His ability to articulate the truths of Scripture is profound, yet his delivery is accessible across cultural contexts. His is a needed voice in our time as one who combats error, points to the truth of Scripture, and exalts Christ."

—PASTOR WILLIAM MCDOWELL, lead pastor at Deeper Fellowship Church

"Far too many churches are experiencing the invasion of an artificial, counterfeit identity and mission. My friend Eric Mason's timely book is a call to scrape away the cultural 'barnacles' that have latched on to the church and realign the Bride of Christ to its beautiful, biblical identity and mission in the world. Thank you, Eric, for the gift of *Rebranding the Church*, a clear, compelling pathway forward."

—DR. CRAWFORD W. LORITTS, JR., author, speaker, radio host, founder and president of Beyond Our Generation

REBRANDING
THE
CHURCH

REBRANDING

THE

CHURCH

RESTORING THE IMAGE OF GOD'S
PEOPLE IN THE WORLD

ERIC MASON

MULTNOMAH

Multnomah
An imprint of the Penguin Random House Christian Publishing Group,
a division of Penguin Random House LLC
1745 Broadway, New York, NY 10019

waterbrookmultnomah.com
penguinrandomhouse.com

Library of Congress Cataloging-in-Publication Data
Names: Mason, Eric (Eric M.), author.
Title: Rebranding the church: restoring the image of God's people in the world / Eric Mason. Description: First edition. | Colorado Springs: Multnomah, [2025] | Includes bibliographical references.
Identifiers: LCCN 2024056896 | ISBN 9780593602119 (hardcover) | ISBN 9780593602133 (ebook)
Subjects: LCSH: Jesus Christ—Example. | Christian life.
Classification: LCC BT304.2 .M3363 2025 | DDC 232.9/04—dc23/eng/20250106
LC record available at https://lccn.loc.gov/2024056896

Printed in the United States of America on acid-free paper

1st Printing

First Edition

The authorized representative in the EU for product safety and compliance is Penguin Random House Ireland, Morrison Chambers, 32 Nassau Street, Dublin D02 YH68, Ireland. https://eu-contact.penguin.ie

BOOK TEAM: Managing editor: Julia Wallace • Production manager: Kevin Garcia • Copy editors: Cara Iverson, Rachel Kirsch • Proofreaders: Drew Goter, Carrie Krause

Book design by Debbie Glasserman

For details on special quantity discounts for bulk purchases, contact specialmarketscms@penguinrandomhouse.com.

To my church, Epiphany Fellowship. Your commitment to the charge of rebranding the church in the world brings my heart joy. Let the saga continue. Let's ride.

CONTENTS

REBRANDING
THE
CHURCH

1

WHAT DO YOU THINK OF WHEN YOU HEAR THE WORD *CHURCH*?

WHAT DO YOU THINK OF WHEN YOU HEAR THE WORD *BASKETBALL*? What do you think of when you hear the word Philadelphia? What do you think of when you hear NewYork? BMW? North Pole?

What do you think of when you hear the word church? Many today think of the church as full of hypocritical, fake, phony, self-righteous, out-of-touch, unloving, judgmental, absent, and self-ish people. Even for those who reject Jesus, the church should still be recognized for some basic things that could garner respect in most settings: love, generosity, philanthropy, patience, and a basic sense of justice. The church should be full of kind, empa-thetic, nurturing, responsible, responsive, and sacrificial people. However, sadly, I think the world has some legitimate problems with us of because of weeds we've been sowing. As the church of Jesus Christ, we have sown much of the former rather than the latter. I'm not saying that the latter characteristics don't exist; I am saying that the negative ones seem to be predominant in the eyes of a non-Christian world.

Problems in the church make headlines every week: Christian nationalism, the foibles of prosperity-gospel preachers, and sex scandals. Add to this the fact that so many Christians define themselves by what they are against rather than what they are for and it is clear the church has a public relations problem. Our brand is calculated by our failures rather than our successes. When you say you are a Christian, people will want you to prove it. Christians are seen as wholesale hypocrites.

Even in the black community, where the church has historically been held in high regard, things are looking grim. For many of us African Americans, Christianity is viewed as the religion of our oppressors. Teachings like "Love your enemies" and passages on slavery are believed to be man-made laws to get black people to become docile slaves of our white so-called superiors. A recent Pew Research Center article called "Faith Among Black Americans" shows that millennials and Gen Zs aren't monolithic when it comes to faith, religion, and spirituality. One of the most interesting facts is that both groups are less connected to the church than past generations, particularly predominantly black churches:

> Protestantism has long dominated the Black American religious landscape, and still does. The survey shows that two-thirds of Black Americans (66%) are Protestant, 6% are Catholic and 3% identify with other Christian faiths—mostly Jehovah's Witnesses. Another 3% belong to non-Christian faiths, the most common of which is Islam.
>
> But about one-in-five Black Americans (21%) are not affiliated with any religion and instead identify as atheist, agnostic or "nothing in particular," and this phenomenon is increasing by generation: Roughly three-in-ten Black Gen Zers (28%) and Millennials (33%) in the survey are religiously unaffiliated,

compared with just 11% of Baby Boomers and 5% of those in the Silent Generation.[1]

Those stats paint a picture of new generations departing the church, but there is a remnant that God is raising up to represent the reign of Jesus effectively on the planet. The gospel is invincible. The stats do not have the last word; however, they should light a fire under followers of Jesus to help the church recover its passion for true discipleship and a more Christlike brand identity.

Today, when seeking to share the good news about Jesus, many times I have to wade through people's hangups with the church before I can get to the gospel. Let me share an example of an issue I've encountered recently.

There is a group known as the Black Conscious Community that is always telling the church what we should be doing. They are a non-monolithic group of black people who value and even worship black identity but hate the church. The community is comprised of black atheists, Kemetics, Black Hebrew Israelites, Moors, Nation of Islam (NOI), and the Five Percent Nation of Islam. Each group is distinct, but they all have a lot in common: They believe that Christianity is the white man's religion, black people are the original man on the planet, and the white man is the devil. This community spends more than half their time trying to debunk and discredit the church. Not all their issues with the church are well researched, but their criticisms have caused people to become disgusted with the church. Although there are many churches doing the Lord's work, it is clear that's not how the church is perceived by and large.

NOI's Louis Farrakhan once challenged the church not to be bought by the government. Many Black nationalists today claim that churches having 501(c)(3) (nonprofit) status means those churches are subject to the government and cannot speak truth to power. Other people, such as the author of the 2016 article "Why Black Churches Are Doing a $11.5 Billion Disservice to the Black Community," generally state that the black church is the wealthiest business in the black community and should be doing more for its community.[2]

With our own internal issues as the universal church, false propaganda from various groups and individuals, and legitimate critiques leveled at the church from within and without, one thing is clear: The church no longer has a healthy reputation. And that poor reputation is keeping the church from effectively accomplishing its mission.

RECENT CHALLENGES

Over the past few years, there has been an inordinate number of idols that have raised their heads and caused the church to lose its footing. On several fronts, the church—in its various spheres, tribes, and philosophies—has become divided over politics and ethics. I wasn't around in the 1960s, but many of my mentors say that now is the most politicized the church has been in decades. While there are many people who believe the church should stay completely out of politics, I am not one of them. I believe we are called to shine the light of Jesus Christ in every sector of society. The apostle Paul encouraged Titus to teach believers that honorable political engagement is a part of the church's witness: "Remind them to submit to rulers and authorities, to obey, to be ready for every good work" (Titus 3:1). But that isn't what we are discussing here. I am concerned about what I would call political idolatry. Both those committed to Christian nationalism and those committed to extreme liberation theology or progressive theologies tend to place too much stock in politics. Tim Keller states this best:

> One of the signs that an object is functioning as an idol is that fear becomes one of the chief characteristics of life. When we center our lives on the idol, we become dependent on it. If our counterfeit god is threatened in any way, our response is complete panic. We do not say, "What a shame, how difficult," but rather "This is the end! There's no hope!"[3]

Each side seems to equate the political success of a particular party as almost an ultimate goal of God. Each side sees the other as fundamentally opposed to God in their voting. I'm around people who believe that if you vote for Donald Trump, you are a sellout whose ultimate allegiance is not to God and you don't care about morality or the welfare of women. Similarly, there are those who believe that if you vote Democrat, you don't care about the unborn. Both are unfair sentiments. Each side has played a major role in affecting the world's view of the church. Christian nationalism has viewed itself as helping the West remain Christian (as if it ever were). The question we need to address is this: What Christianity are we talking about? A form of cultural imperialism wrapped in Christian clothing? In other words, the Christian faith for nationalists requires patriotism to the United States. There's nothing wrong with healthy patriotism. However, patriotism is not required of Jesus followers, and just because someone is a patriot doesn't mean they are a believer.

Too many professing Christians

> treat faith and citizenship as a package deal, which lulls us toward nationalistic pseudo-Christianity and allows those with no cred-

ible Christian devotion to self-identify as evangelical. Partisan values now define American evangelicalism. Votes in a national election can weigh as heavily as a genuine confession of faith. Because the bar is so low, masqueraders are polled and licensed to speak representatively—marring the evangelical image.[4]

On the more progressive end, there can be efforts to remove aspects of tradition that are good for society in general. For example, consider how gender ideology is currently bringing confusion into spaces where distinctions between male and female have long been clear. What's concerning about progressive ideologies is that everything can, at times, seem up for grabs to be redefined or terminated, even helpful norms and definitions:

> Conservative and progressive are notions that once existed independent of political parties. As we will see, there were conservatives and progressives in both parties. "Conservatism" refers to the desire to maintain the social status quo or return to a social norm from a previous generation. Progressivism is the assumption that society should be in a constant state of social evolution, arguing that societal change is evidence of a healthy community.[5]

Each sector culturally infuses Christianity with their chosen ideologies. Both are guilty of creating a pseudo-Christianity. They both use the Christian name and rhetoric, but neither represents biblical Christianity. Christian nationalism is Americanism; Christ isn't central—America is. Similarly, many hyper-progressive ideologies replace Jesus with a false sense of freedom. Both view their desired ends as a savior and believe we are doomed if the opposite political preferences are represented in government.

How does that affect our witness? When Christ is not center

stage, the world is robbed of experiencing the true gospel. That also tells us something about the church: It has lost its saltiness. Personal preferences have overridden God's biblical principles. For that and much more, our witness has diminished.

Moreover, the world has seen its fair share of impudent examples of "faith." As a result, there has been a decline in expectations of the church to be what she's supposed to be.

I want to help you, assuming you are a Christian, be intentional about taking responsibility for acting as a healthy gospel witness in the world. Speaking of health, I mean painting a true biblical picture of the people of God that represents His intended purposes in the world. Peter urged believers to be intentional about cultivating their reputation in a nonbelieving world (see 1 Peter 2:11–12).

God has placed the responsibility of cultivating a good reputation for the church on the shoulders of every believer. When we trust Jesus, we are automatically drafted into representing our team.

IT'S GOING TO GET WORSE BEFORE IT GETS BETTER

There was a time in redemptive history when things did get better rather quickly. Prior to the establishment of the church, the spiritual condition of God's people experienced a downward spiral. Between the Fall in Genesis 3 and the evil of Genesis 6, we don't see much change until Noah comes onto the scene. During the time of the judges, things deteriorate, and then the time of the kings is a bit of a roller coaster, but overall God's people seem to be moving in the wrong direction. Things get better and then worse again while God's people are living in captivity. And then Jesus comes and ushers in a new era of history.

The initial church that Jesus gave birth to through His death, resurrection, and ascension was quite remarkable. The members of the early church were attentive to the teaching they received; they loved and supported one another and sought to live out the teachings of Jesus (see Acts 2:42–47). I believe there are many communities of believers still striving to live this way, but these communities just don't make headlines. My point here, however, is that there have always been seasons of pruning—times when God allows the church to suffer to some degree so she can grow to be more like Jesus. I think we are in one of those seasons right now and, by remembering the church's past, we can look to God to lead us toward a brighter future.

THE PRUNING

In the book of John, Jesus makes a statement about how the kingdom best grows and bears fruit: "Every branch in me that does not produce fruit he removes, and he prunes every branch that produces fruit so that it will produce more fruit" (15:2). The word for *prune* here means "to cleanse"; the adjective "'clean' (*katharos*) is occasionally used in Greek literature in connection with the growth of vines."[6] Also, this verse should be read more corporately than individually. Although by application it could be a personal point of sanctification, it refers more to Israel as the people of God and will apply to the church later. Pruning is so important for things to thrive, both corporately and individually:

> Those tending vines (and some kinds of trees) would cut away useless branches lest they wastefully sap the strength of the plant; in the long run, this diverted more strength into the branches that would genuinely bear fruit. The weaker the vine, the more harshly one pruned it, reducing short-term fruit but ensuring a greater measure of fruit the following year. Farmers

pruned in two different ways: they pruned fruitful branches to make them more fruitful, and (as in 15:6) they removed un-fruitful branches entirely.[7]

In light of this, I have been seeking God through all the loss my church experienced during the pandemic (many people left our church and never came back). I noticed the same with other churches as well. John 15:2 seemed to be what the Lord was using to give me clarity on what He was providentially working on among His people.

I want to talk about three types of pruning that I believe all churches are going through and will continue to go through in the future. I will explain each as we go:

- Leadership pruning
- Local church member pruning
- Local church lampstand pruning

Leadership Pruning

I'm not going into full detail here because I'll speak on leadership later, but there will be a cleansing of leadership. For far too long, the church has harbored unclean and uncalled people to remain in leadership positions, from abusers and whoremongers to greedy, manipulative, immature, materialistic, controlling, cultic, non-Bible-teaching, non-gospel-centered, non-Christ-centered, idolatrous leaders. Those types of leaders are going to be pruned out of the church of Jesus Christ. For years, leaders have been propagating a mess that God has patiently tolerated. However, a time is approaching when countless scandals will emerge, expos-ing those leaders. Some may even go home to be with the Lord earlier than expected. Others might be exposed as never having been called or saved at all.

Local Church Member Pruning

As stated earlier, many churches lost numerous attendees and members from 2020 to 2022. While there are certainly other reasons, I primarily attribute this to cleansing. God wants a serious group representing His reign. The church I pastor, Epiphany Fellowship Church, lost 75 percent of its people. During the pandemic, our leaders called every member of our church to see if anyone needed anything and how we could serve them. Some responded, and others didn't. When we reopened, I was deeply saddened by how many members we seemed to have lost. Not everyone who didn't return to our church completely left the church or abandoned their faith in Jesus, but something odd happened concerning people's relationship with the church during and after the pandemic.

As I write this, I can say that we are on the other side of the pruning season. We are experiencing exponential growth and seeing many new converts and baptisms. God has been gracious, and I believe He isn't nearly done helping us bear fruit. I have heard of other pastors and churches experiencing some of the same fruit that we are. God is amazing!

Local Church Lampstand Pruning

In Revelation 2, John says, "I have this against you: You have abandoned the love you had at first. Remember then how far you have fallen; repent, and do the works you did at first. Otherwise, I will come to you and remove your lampstand from its place, unless you repent" (verses 4–5). Every local church has a lampstand lit in heaven that represents its presence on earth. As long as it is lit, the church serves as a viable outpost of the kingdom. But if the lampstand is not lit, the church is no longer God's ordained representative. Churches may have lost their representation, but they haven't lost their salvation.

The church at Ephesus was sound in doctrine but unsound in love—and as John warned them, "You have abandoned the love you had at first." The church today is in danger of losing its first love. Abandoning our first love isn't just about neglecting Bible reading and devotional life; it is about our affection for God and people, from pastoral care to mercy ministry to doing all things motivated by humility and love.

There are so many churches out there that fight good pastors and run them off. Other churches are controlled by founding or core families who resist the gospel mission and want to return the church to its "glory days" or keep the status quo; many pastors stay long beyond their time and effectiveness in hopes of helping advance God's mission and making disciples. Other churches have had diminished presence in their community; many don't even have websites. Their Facebook page is their website. If Paul used letters, ships, donkeys, and Roman roads to continue sharing the gospel, why aren't we using whatever redemptive means we have available to do the same? It will look different for churches of varying sizes, but we are called to be gospel innovators to advocate for the rule of Christ on earth. In my city alone, I've seen numerous churches go out of existence or sell their facilities.

David Kinnaman, CEO of Barna Group, believes that "the sense of deep-rooted connectedness that most Americans have to a local church is becoming more and more transactional, less and less frequent."[8] Kinnaman said that the first year and a half of the pandemic "didn't just change how Christians met; it changed their hearts and minds toward the church."[9] In its research on the state of the church, Barna Group found that

a third of practicing Christians had dropped out of church at some point and 29 percent of senior pastors said they "seriously considered" quitting in the past year.[10]

And Kinnaman said,

> Church leaders are going to revert to doing things the ways they've always known them, whereas the population in general and millennials are going to find that this disruption altered their habits and perspectives on the role and relevance of the church . . . The gap between the church and society is only going to be larger as we rebuild the church in a postpandemic world.[11]

Although I know all this is necessary for kingdom growth, it's painful. However, I do believe that God is distilling us down to a remnant of people who are what they were saved to be: representatives. Remember, the church of Jesus Christ was a remnant. Most Israelites rejected Jesus, and the multitudes called for Him to be crucified. But only 120 disciples were at Pentecost, and after the Resurrection, Jesus appeared to more than 500 believers (see Acts 1:15; 1 Corinthians 15:6). The church started with a few, but the gospel moved quickly to thousands. God doesn't need a crowd; He can use a small community.

THE CHURCH MUST BE CLEAR ON WHO JESUS IS

I believe the church currently finds herself in an identity crisis. Many Christians are struggling to discover who they are again; others are trying to recreate the church and restore her back to the way she was, but she will never be the same. I believe the way forward is both backward and forward. What I mean by backward is that we need to recapture the essence of what the church is biblically meant to be. That is a timeless task we will explore later, but it's important we recognize that, in changing times, the truth of God's Word will never change. And the gospel will never change.

WHAT DO YOU THINK OF WHEN YOU HEAR THE WORD *CHURCH*?

But we are also to move forward: While the gospel never changes, we ourselves must change. We must constantly ask ourselves how we can live more faithfully for Jesus in the unique context in which God has placed us.

Jesus asked many questions during His ministry. His questions are worthy of a sermon series. Perhaps the most important question He asked was this: "Who do you say that I am?" (Matthew 16:15). Before that question, He asked the second-most-important question of His ministry: "Who do people say that the Son of Man is?" (verse 13). We will deal with that one first.

The second question Jesus asked His disciples assumes at least three things. The first is that Christians interact with culture. He said, "I am not praying that you take them out of the world but that you protect them from the evil one" (John 17:15). Jesus wants His disciples insulated but not isolated. He expected His followers to be engaged and involved in human flourishing.

Second, He knows that He'll be talked about. In light of that, He believes that we'll have an answer or at least notice when others misrepresent Him. Third is the expectation that His disciples were listening and perceiving what people's take on Him was. "Imbedded in Jesus's question is the answer. I wonder if the disciples caught it: 'the Son of Man.' 'Son of Man' is a title, Jesus was referring to Daniel 7:13–14 where the prophet Daniel 'described a ruler of heavenly origin who would reign over a universal and eternal kingdom. It was Jesus's favorite self-designation and, in fact, is used approximately thirty times in Matthew alone.'"[12]

When Jesus asked His disciples, "Who do people say that the Son of Man is?" (Matthew 16:13), He didn't ask them this question in Jerusalem; He asked them in pagan territory. It's easy to say who Jesus is in church and around believers, but it is a challenge to stand for Him in places of resistance.

In the context of Matthew's gospel, "At the time Jesus and his disciples traveled there, Caesarea Philippi was an important Greco-Roman city, whose population was primarily pagan. This region becomes the site where Jesus calls for a decision about his own identity and where it is revealed by the Father to Peter that Jesus is truly the prophesied divine Messiah."[13]

It seems the disciples were listening, as they had a list of people who had heard about Jesus, many of whom had experienced Him in real time. It's possible to encounter Jesus and still not be able to process who He is. That is why we as believers need to have clarity on who He is. The disciples replied, "Some say John the Baptist; others, Elijah; still others, Jeremiah or one of the prophets" (Matthew 16:14).

> All these answers about who Jesus is fall into the "prophets" category; though most Jewish teachers held that prophets had ceased, popular expectation of end-time prophets remained strong. Elijah was expected to return (Mal 4:5), and many of Jesus' miracles resembled Elijah's. His judgment oracles (Mt 11:20–24) or downplaying the temple (cf. 12:6; 24:1–2) may have evoked the comparison with Jeremiah.[14]

We live in a world where most people have a strong opinion about the church, Jesus, and Christianity. We must be clear on who Jesus is; that is fundamental to following Him (see Matthew 16:16–17). As we seek to rebrand the church, we must start with Jesus—by speaking clearly and passionately about who He is and why it matters.

Most people today say that Jesus is a good man, a solid example, a prophet, or a revolutionary. They may even see Him as countercultural in a positive way or the embodiment of love. These are only part of the picture. Most people tend to reduce Jesus down to their favorite parts of who they believe He is. People want Jesus and Christianity and the Bible à la carte. Most people in the world (and even many in the church) have a less-than-biblical under-standing of the true Jesus. My friend Sho Baraka illustrates this in his song "Maybe Both, 1865." Here is a sample stanza:

What's your standard? Where you stand?
What's your views?
What gives you the right to think the way that you do?
Is it school? Is it news?
Is it man's wisdom? Is it religion?
Why listen when you can make your own decisions?
It's funny how some people see the Lord
Some see him as a pacifist
Some see him with a sword
The Lord who hated sin showed grace to the thief
Saved the lonely prostitute from being stoned in the street
He was holy, but he hung with the sinful
Drove the wicked out by flipping over tables in the temple
He took a wrongful death, and yet he remained silent
But he said he coming back, and he is bringing violence
Many people isolate him just to make him fit their cause
Never too involved in a greater context at all
So, are there two Christs totally unrelated
Or, maybe there's one Christ, and he's pretty complicated
Huh? Pretty complicated
Or, maybe it is both
Maybe, it is both
Maybe, both

—SHO BARAKA, "MAYBE BOTH, 1865"

Jesus asked the disciples the million-dollar question: "Who do you say that I am?" (verse 15). Simon Peter answered, "You are the Messiah, the Son of the living God" (verse 16). Peter received supernatural revelation on this, but he didn't fully know what it meant. When we first meet Jesus, we don't know all that we should, but we must be in a position for Him to tell and teach us who He is through the Word, Spirit, and church. Jesus then lets Peter know He didn't come to the conclusion on His own but that the Father graced Him to know that truth. If we hope to rebrand the church, to align the church with the heart of Jesus, we must be crystal clear on who Jesus is.

THE CHURCH DEFINED

The Greek word for church is ekklesia, "which is derived from ek, meaning 'out of,' and kaleo, which means 'to call'; hence, the church is 'a called-out group.'"[15] The church, then, is called out of the world to enter into a relationship with God and other believers, serving as agents of an invisible kingdom to the visible world. The church is a people, not a building. The word refers to local assemblies of Jesus followers all over the world.

We must ask ourselves, what makes a local church a church? Teaching, preaching, evangelism, prayer, worship, love, service, elders, deacons, communion, baptism, and born-again human beings? By the time Paul wrote 1 and 2 Timothy and Titus, there were practices and structures that had to be standard in every church in the world to make it a viable outpost of God's presence on earth.

In terms of rebranding, the products the church has on offer are heavenly in nature. I like to patronize local businesses in North Philly, so I went to a newly opened seafood spot. I looked at the menu, which was amazing. I asked for a seafood salad, and they said they didn't have it. I asked for shrimp, and they said they didn't have it. I asked about the scallops, and they said they didn't have them. I asked, "What do you have, then?" They said that all they had was chicken and fish. I then thanked them and walked out. That establishment didn't have in stock what they advertised, so they should have just been called something like "So-and-So's Chicken and Fish." Many churches participate in false advertising. They say they have forgiveness, but they only have bitterness. They say they have holiness, but only whoremongers abide. They say they have love, but there is vicious backbiting. They say they have kindness, but they are overrun with cliques.

Jesus stated, "On this rock I will build my church, and the gates of Hades will not overpower it" (Matthew 16:18). The Catholic church views the rock as Peter and the papal succession as the Rock many Protestants believe that Jesus is. However, remember that Jesus is in Caesarea Philippi. The fact that He chose this location to ask His disciples who He is and tell them He will build His church is very telling.

The late Michael S. Heiser states,

There's actually something much more cosmic going on here. The location of the incident—Caesarea Philippi—and the reference to the "gates of hell" provide the context for the "rock" of which Jesus is speaking. The location of Caesarea Philippi should be familiar from our earlier discussions about the wars against the giant clans.[16]

Jesus is talking about locations of darkness. He went to one of the darkest locations on the planet at that time. This was seen as the devil's front door, and He says the gates of hell won't be able to stop the things that God wants to do through His church. Jesus was establishing God's kingdom on earth and profoundly declaring that Satan would not stop Him. Christ's church, from its prophetic inception, was always supposed to be, like Jesus, declaring truth in places of darkness.

The church needs to incarnate in culture. We gather and we scatter! We should be a community of communities, a city within cities. The calling of the church is to incarnate the life of Jesus into society as viable gospel witnesses and represent God's reign on earth.

Our light must find its way into the structures of society. The church must be fluid in form but firm in function. What makes us the church never changes, but the way we live out our identity as the church might. Jesus wants us to display the unchanging truth of His Word to the structures of the world. In other words, we are supposed to be mobile lights. We are to go into the arts, business, education, government, the marketplace, agriculture, medicine, and sports. We do that in our vocation, and we also do it in "third places."

In missiology terms, third places are the places where we want to chill, relax, and have fun. First place is home, and second place is work. Those are places you have to be, but a third place is where you desire to build relationships and engage people without any formal responsibility. Examples are coffee shops, sporting leagues, digital media, entertainment and resort venues, and pubs. "Next generations such as Generation X, Millennials, and Generation [Z] especially orient their lives around these third places. Many of us have friends who inhabit coffee shops every day of the week, participate in running groups every weekend without exception, and form community in online relationships daily."[17]

The Enemy will try but won't be able to overpower the church, from the gates Jesus moves to the keys that open the gates. The gates are what the enemy puts in place of God's work through the church to limit kingdom movement. "Keys" in the ancient world symbolized access to power and the ability to open the doors to the heavenly realms. The main function of the keys is admittance in Christ's kingdom for those gated in the Enemy's kingdom. The keys aren't singular; they're plural, meaning there are many things they can unlock.

What are these keys? The promises of God Himself:

1. The Gospel (Acts 1:8) = Unlocks Souls
2. The Name of Jesus (John 14:12–14) = Unlocks Obstacles
3. Spiritual Weapons (2 Corinthians 10:3–6) = Unlock Spiritual Power
4. Spiritual Gifts (Romans 12:3–8; 1 Corinthians 12:1–11; Ephesians 4:4–16) = Unlock Growth
5. Spiritual Governance (1 Corinthians 5) = Unlocks Order
6. The Promises of God (2 Corinthians 1:20) = Unlock Resources

These keys are God's means through church to override things happening on earth. While riding in the car, my kids are always telling me when the light has turned green. One such day, the light turned green, but I didn't push the gas pedal, so my daughter said, "Daddy, the light is green. You can go now." I told her, "You hear that sound? It's the police." She asked, "How come they don't follow the rules?" I explained that they do but that when there is an emergency, they have been authorized by a higher authority to turn their lights on and sound the alarm and siren. Everyone else must stop or get out of their way. They have been authorized to supersede the normal law. Likewise, the keys Jesus has given to the church have given us the ability to supersede and unlock the normal for the supernatural.

There is some stuff that God won't unlock in isolation, so to be disconnected from the church community is to lack connection to the keys. The keys are held by us, not you—we, not me. You aren't the church by yourself; *we* are the church. It is a community of believers, and God uses community to deepen our faith and launch us into the world on mission for Him.

We mustn't give up on God's renewing our witness to the world. In the pages of this work, I'd like to present to you some key factors that we, as the church, need to take seriously, because as of now, we have lost quite a bit of ground. It is time for us to view ourselves as a gospel remnant to restore our witness and represent the reign of Christ in this lost world.

The church is an ancient yet timeless movement; it's not one that needs to be started anew. This movement started on the Day of Pentecost, and it was more than a once-a-week gathering. The church was a people who were called out by God to participate in a renewed community—a people who believed that He is in the business of changing and redeeming everything. Redeeming just points to God's getting His creation back in line with His created intentions. By leaning into Him and His design for the church, we will discover His intention for friendship, marriage, single-ness, happiness, purpose, enjoyment, sacrifice, and love, as well as how you love and serve others and how you view family, money and generosity, gender, and yourself. What we are talking about in this book isn't new; it's ancient and beautiful and life-giving. It's a whole vibe!

2

BRAND AMBASSADORS

NOW MORE THAN EVER, PEOPLE NEED TO SEE THE GOSPEL LIVED out by those who believe it. Underlying all the church hate that people are expressing today is a cry for us, the real children of God, to show our faces and be who He has called us to be. This comes through how we speak, do business, treat one another, live, repent, teach and preach, serve, and build healthy families. It is important to see the implications of the gospel in every area of our lives, but we must ask ourselves if that is what the world sees.

A church in Detroit recently had its worship service interrupted by a group called New Era Detroit (NED), an advocacy group that seeks to improve underserved black communities at a fundamental level. Few would disagree with their purpose, which is an honorable one.

However, NED members showed up to the Sunday morning service of Greater Faith Ministries (GFM). One of the NED members charged the pulpit. Apparently, GFM had recently invited Donald Trump to speak to the church. That was all NED needed to justify their protest. A fight broke out in the church and went viral. (When foolish or dangerous things happen at church, they go viral.)

In the minds of the NED, their protest was a prophetic call to serve the community. NED spoke out against the pastor of GFM. They claimed the pastor made a ton of money on the backs of the underserved community while flaunting his accumulated wealth in its face. Seeing a leader driving a Rolls-Royce and living in a mansion while the community suffers didn't make sense. To them, it was hypocrisy at the highest level. That kind of flaunting of wealth by pastors is nothing new. I recently saw another pastor in a different state post a picture on social media of his Bentley parked next to the church. His luxury car costs $230,000—significantly more than the median price of a home in the neighborhood surrounding his church.

I'm not one to say a pastor can't have nice things, but when something becomes a stumbling block to gospel mission, I think we should slow down, search our hearts, and maybe take a long hard look in the mirror. In recent years, an Instagram page called "Preachers and Sneakers" contains reports on the cost of various prominent American pastors' clothing and kicks. If you need more evidence of the propensity of modern preachers to flaunt their wealth, check out that Instagram page and take note of the cost of the outfits some pastors choose to wear on a regular basis. The comments section is riddled with opinions from believers and unbelievers alike. Anyone who knows me understands I love a great sneaker, but I want to be careful of anything that eclipses the glory of God. It seems that many leaders don't care or else have other values.

With this in mind, people have a passion for the church to be more engaged with the underserved, speak prophetically to power, and be an example of what Jesus teaches. That's fair. Although many people may have never read the Bible, they have a sense that Christians should be different—better than they seem to be. When we do something out of pocket, someone might say, "I thought you were a Christian!" They know inherently that we are supposed to represent something countercultural. Mostly what people see from the church in local communities is gathering and leaving. In other words, many people do not see churches doing much to serve the people of the community. Just peruse any number of forums on social media where people talk about the church, and you will notice that we are seen as opinionated and not loving or gracious. And I'm not even referring to politics!

When a church collaborates with local police to start a boxing program for three hundred youths and young adults to benefit the neighborhoods around their church, no one seems to care or pay attention. And when a church has an outreach that serves three thousand people and helps them get jobs, health screenings, and free clothes and haircuts, that will grab hardly a hundred views on social media. But the reality is that if two people knuckle up in the church or the preacher is found in some scandal, you're going to rack up five billion views because our culture is obsessed with mess.

The world loves it when the church takes an L, and what's interesting to me is how some people think that all churches are illegitimate, as if this is the brand identity of the entirety of the people of God. But what hurts me most is not how we are perceived by the world; my concern is how so many who profess to follow Jesus have the same sour sentiments as people outside the church. And I wonder if there will be a day when God will raise the standard in our minds of who we are and what we're supposed to do. Will we ever mature to the point where when the word church comes up, it's not a byword for hypocritical but rather a blessed word? I want church to go from a messy word to a ministry one. I want it to go from a foul word to a faithful one.

When we talk about rebranding, we're not talking about creating something new; we're talking about returning to and magnifying what's been true for more than two thousand years. *Branding* refers to the distinctive wording or design that is used to help people easily identify something and where it came from. It's the promotion of a particular product or company by means of advertising and unique design. It's also "the marketing practice of creating a name, symbol or design that identifies and differentiates a product from other products."[1]

Conversely, *rebranding* is the process of changing the corporate image of an organization. It is a market strategy of giving a new name, symbol, or change in design for an already established brand. "The goal of rebranding is to create a new and differentiated brand identity in the minds of consumers, investors, prospects, competitors, employees, and the general public."[2] So, when I assert that the church needs rebranding, I mean the church needs to be "re-presented." I am not saying the church needs a new veneer or a new coat of paint. Rebranding is only truly effective when the outside matches the inside. The church needs to know who she is, engage the world, and represent the name of Jesus well in the world. Scripture is filled with examples of how God wants His people to represent His name and reproduce His image. Genesis 1 is the first of the Great Commission passages.

God blessed His people and then said, "Be fruitful, multiply, fill the earth, and subdue it" (Genesis 1:28). The next Great Commission passage is Genesis 9:1: "God blessed Noah and his sons and said to them, 'Be fruitful and multiply and fill the earth.'" After that, God speaks to Abraham in Genesis 12 and 17, where He promises that He will bless all nations through Abraham and Sarah. Later, we see God's intention for Israel to be a kingdom of priests who spread His ways to the nations. In Matthew 28:18–20, Jesus restates this mission to His disciples, which is an ancient mission passed down through redemptive history for all the people of God to take on.

WHY REBRANDING IS NECESSARY

As I've stated, the church has been branded badly in the world. Everything from movies over the past fifty-plus years to social media today is a fiasco when it comes to who we Christians are and what we are supposed to do. We have done a less-than-ideal job ourselves, and non-Christians often pounce on those faults whenever they can. We give them fodder, but the Enemy initiates his own smear campaigns as well. In the blaxploitation films of the 1970s, pastors were rarely painted in a good light. In those films, it is as if all pastors are crooks, liars, and womanizers. Today, even saying you are a pastor doesn't come with dignity and a sense of value and integrity. In my experience, it comes with the baggage of bad expectations. This said, we mustn't become shy or ashamed of being the people of God. Our call is to set a new tone through repentance and representation.

In short, all God's people are called to be brand ambassadors. What do I mean by *brand ambassadors?* A brand ambassador is a person (especially a celebrity) who is paid to endorse or promote a particular company's products or services. However, that definition leaves out the most important characteristic of brand ambassadorship: a strong relationship with a brand.

A brand ambassador is someone who promotes your brand on a long-term basis. They represent your brand values and showcase who you are through a number of consumer touchpoints. Their success is down to their ability to share authentic recommendations built from the ongoing relationship they have developed with your brand. And this makes them a valuable asset, provided you understand the brand ambassador meaning, in all its forms, and follow the right strategy.[3]

Responsibilities of brand ambassadors include, but are not limited to, the following:

- Representing the brand positively in a multitude of settings
- Assisting in content creation (i.e., writing blogs, newsletters, product reviews, etc.)
- Participating in event marketing
- Generating brand awareness through word-of-mouth marketing
- Being an opinion leader in his/her community
- Providing feedback and insight on new products/services
- Promoting the brand via his personal social media accounts[4]

Although this is a corporate analogy, it fits well with the fact that we as believers are to represent the brand of the glory of God well. Above, you saw what is generally expected for those who represent brands. Responsibilities of ambassadors of Christ include, but are not limited to, the following:

- Representing Jesus positively in all settings
- Assisting in using all redeemable means to communicate Him clearly to the world
- Participating in community outreach with other believers
- Generating awareness through word-of-mouth communication
- Being faith leaders in their communities

- Providing feedback and insight into other ways to present the truth
- Promoting the kingdom through all helpful public means

It's best when brand ambassadors love and naturally enjoy the products they represent. That is why Scripture calls us "ambassadors for Christ":

We are ambassadors for Christ, since God is making his appeal through us. We plead on Christ's behalf, "Be reconciled to God." (2 Corinthians 5:20)

"An 'ambassador' was a representative of one state to another, usually applied in this period to the emperor's legates in the East."[5] As believers, our "product" is the gospel. I am not intending to reduce the gospel to a mere product, but it is what we represent more than anything else. The great thing about this product is that although it was an expense to God, it is free to us. We receive all the benefits as a free gift.

BRAND AMBASSADORS NEED CLARITY AND EMPOWERMENT

Acts 1 marks the ending of Jesus's earthly ministry. He is about to ascend to heaven. Prior to this ascension, He communicated with His disciples about the main thing they would need to focus on while He was gone, which was being His witnesses. But before that, He began a refresher course for them: "While he was with them, he commanded them not to leave Jerusalem, but to wait for the Father's promise. 'Which,' he said, 'you have heard me speak about'" (Acts 1:4). I love that, because Jesus, at this point, has been with His disciples post-resurrection for forty days. And He has been re-engaging with them about what He had taught them over three years. He gave them such an information dump that the book of John, in its final chapter, says, "If every one of them were written down, I suppose not even the world itself could contain the books that would be written" (21:25). As a matter of fact, the earth isn't a big enough library to contain the record of everything Jesus did to show the disciples that He was the Christ. He spent all that time trying to teach them brand clarity to make sure everyone would be on the same page.

Before Jesus gives them their assignment and purpose, He assures them of their empowerment. Before He sends out His ambassadors, like any good brand trainer, He gives them an orientation. This orientation is the preamble to their representing Him without His personal, human, physical presence with them. He promises to be with them in another way: through a co-equal and co-eternal person of the Trinity called the Holy Spirit.

In the book of Acts, we're told, "John baptized with water, but you will be baptized with the Holy Spirit in a few days" (1:5). And the Spirit doesn't fill you like water; what He does is take control, in partnership with you, to represent Jesus. True brand ambassadors for Christ are filled with the Spirit as their personal lives are submitted to God, resulting in the edification of other believers as well as advancing His mission in the world.

CAN I GET A WITNESS?

Although the gospel is the power of God for salvation (Romans 1:16, NIV), the early church needed empowerment and authority as the ones who would be Jesus's ambassadors. There are many barriers to the gospel in the world, such as suffering, false information, and warfare from the Enemy. These barriers inform us of an important need we all have: divine power. We need the Spirit to empower us to overcome the many challenges we will face in our efforts as brand ambassadors for Christ.

Recently, I led an Iranian Muslim to Jesus and later had the privilege of baptizing him. He knew very little English; however, he could understand enough to hear and respond to the gospel. He had been a Muslim his whole life. Because I was familiar with apologetics, I could answer his questions, but he needed the power that accompanies the gospel. Having the power of the Spirit also helps us personally in the journey of being a brand ambassador.

The most important need for empowerment is boldness. The focus of empowerment is to be witnesses, meaning actually sharing the faith. Jesus lays out the way this faith will grow: It will go global. The Holy Spirit brings heaven to earth in the church so the church can bring heaven to the world. We tend to reduce the role of the Holy Spirit to our church gatherings, but the main reason for Jesus's presence in the lives of believers is for us to be His witnesses.

Your witness matters more than you know. Being a witness is both verbal and nonverbal. Most times, the nonverbal precedes the verbal. My wife is the sweetest person on earth, and not just to me but to so many others. In one of her numerous stays in the hospital, the doctors, nurses, and techs became fond of her. Her candor and demeanor under harsh trials bewildered them. They would speak of their other patients experiencing similar or less severe circumstances who gave them the business and weren't as tolerant. In light of her disposition, she was able to pray for and minister to some of the staff and teams that came to her hospital room. Her Christlike attitude gave her the right to be heard.

PURPOSE VERSUS ASSIGNMENT

Today, you will hear many messages about purpose. Whether in reels on Facebook and Instagram or in shorts on YouTube, messages about purpose are in heavy rotation on the algorithm. When it comes to churches with a focus on younger generations, it is clear they believe that those messages lead to connection and growth. Many times, purpose involves business, wealth, talent, or gifting that one can monetize. However, none of these get at our deepest purpose, our God-given purpose, which God defines in His Word. By *purpose*, I mean the larger goals He has in the world based on His divine will. He "works all things after the counsel of His will."[6] God has large goals that He wants to get done, and nothing we do can thwart them. And God invites us to participate in His goals— namely, to represent Him to the world, to point people to Jesus.

Being witnesses of God is one of the fundamental purposes we have as disciples. Our purpose, however, is not merely personal but also communal. We are called as the church to represent Jesus together, a community of witnesses all pointing to the glory and goodness of Jesus. Anything personal can be called an assignment, but all our assignments must in some way connect to God's will and must honor His intended ends. Let's explore a few Bible verses about purpose:

David, after serving God's purpose in his own generation, fell asleep, [and] was buried with his fathers. (Acts 13:36)

I consider my life of no value to myself; my purpose is to finish my course and the ministry I received from the Lord Jesus, to testify to the gospel of God's grace. (20:24)

[I am] a minister of Christ Jesus to the Gentiles, serving as a priest of the gospel of God. God's purpose is that the Gentiles may be an acceptable offering, sanctified by the Holy Spirit. (Romans 15:16)

The purpose was that the blessing of Abraham would come to the Gentiles by Christ Jesus, so that we could receive the promised Spirit through faith. (Galatians 3:14)

He has saved us and called us with a holy calling, not according to our works, but according to his own purpose and grace, which was given to us in Christ Jesus before time began. (2 Timothy 1:9)

You have followed my teaching, conduct, purpose, faith, patience, love, and endurance. (3:10)

Because God wanted to show his unchangeable purpose even more clearly to the heirs of the promise, he guaranteed it with an oath. (Hebrews 6:17)

The one who commits sin is of the devil, for the devil has sinned from the beginning. The Son of God was revealed for this purpose: to destroy the devil's works. (1 John 3:8)

Notice the constant theme of purpose in each of the verses. Our purpose is to be witnesses to God's larger divine plan for and through His people. In essence, our function is to build our lives around God's desired ends. Our problem is we often have a gospel of abundant life that is more self-serving than God glorifying.

I recently surveyed friends of mine who lead in churches about what the people in their communities believe is the church's purpose. I asked them to share both reasonable and unreasonable expectations they've seen firsthand. They said people expect the church to do the following:

- Provide financial support. Some people even believe the church should cover all bills and needs.
- Provide everything under the sun for people's children (life skills, career development, discipleship, every extra-curricular activity).
- Pursue everyone's personal mission, vision, and values.
- Never collect a dime of donations but somehow always have money to give to people in need.
- Be responsive to people's wants and desires.
- Entertain and satisfy any social void people feel.
- Do the heavy lifting of applying God's truth to their lives without their having to take ownership of their spiritual maturity.

When my family joined the YMCA, we looked at all the things we had access to and the services that were provided (swim classes, personal trainer, day care, and so on). We paid the organization, and we expected fulfillment of services. People have a tendency to treat church membership like that: "I invest; therefore, I get to withdraw." People think they are paying (giving and attending) to have their specific needs met. They see their tithes and attendance as payment, so they believe the church is there to serve them as consumers rather than the church serving Christ. In black social circles you hear this a lot from people who grew up in the church or from non-Christians who view giving to the church in transactional terms ("I give to get back"). In reality, the church exists to serve Jesus. Serving Him often involves meeting various needs of people who attend its gatherings, but a consumer mentality misses the bigger and much more beautiful picture of what God created the church to be and do.

It's not earth's job to say or influence how heaven is to operate. No, it is earth's job to find out what heaven wants and be a means to bring it down here. But some of us aren't bringing down heaven; we are literally raising hell.

One of the biggest deterrents to living as brand ambassadors of Christ is divisiveness. Divisiveness always distracts from the mission of God by putting the focus on some side issue. Every occurrence of divisiveness I've dealt with over the past twenty years has fatigued those who are truly about the mission of God. In one of our small groups, some folks began to speak on issues they had in the church. None of this was brought to me or my elders, but rather it was made into a private and ongoing discussion. New believers and new members were looped into these discussions. Thankfully, some mature believers were also looped in and were able to call out the madness. Sadly, one new person left over the debacle. The goal of certain people in the discussion group was not to unify the church by pointing out things the leadership team could grow in or by offering constructive criticism; it seemed their goal was solely to develop a disgruntled base to gain power.

Please hear my heart. I believe that all church leaders should be open to constructive criticism from church members. However, gossip and slander can often be disguised as constructive criticism, and criticism of church leadership is constructive only when it is delivered to the people who can do something about it: leaders. Rebranding the church well requires us all, leaders and members of the church alike, to strive to be Christlike with our words. Private discussion groups dedicated to criticizing the church aren't helping us be more like Jesus.

Whenever you operate on earthly terms, you get earthly results; when you operate on heavenly terms, you get heavenly results. One is natural, and the other is spiritual. Satan likes earth's terms because earth is his playground, but heaven is spiritual and empowered by God. You have to do life on heaven's terms because the Enemy has no power over those. Additionally, remember that you are part of the body of Christ, which means you have a responsibility to care for and support the church: its members, leaders, and structures. This might be a good time to ask God to help you examine your heart with regard to the church: "God, help me love my church well." And if you have criticisms about the way your church operates, ask Him to help you determine which of them need to be voiced to leadership and which are personal preferences or minor grievances that you just need to let go of. If you have important concerns or legitimate hurts, ask God for wisdom about how to voice those concerns in ways that honor Him, show love to your neighbor, and promote the flourishing of Christ's church.

Satan has power in our personal purposes and kingdoms, but he is powerless in the kingdom of Christ and His purposes. Jesus promises that the gates of Hades won't be able to overpower the church. Empowerment is set around our pushing God's kingdom forward through the church. The eagle does not fight the snake on the ground; it lifts it into the sky and changes the battleground, then releases the snake. The snake has no stamina, power, or balance in the air. It is useless, weak, and vulnerable, unlike on the ground, where it is powerful, wise, and deadly. Take your fight into the spiritual realm, where God takes over your battles. Don't fight the Enemy in his comfort zone; change the battlegrounds like the eagle, and let God take charge through you. You'll be assured of a clean victory.

Paul says in Ephesians not to "give the devil an opportunity" (4:27). The word *opportunity* means space, room, and the chance to function or perform. In other words, use the means God has given you: prayer, resistance, the Bible, and counsel from older, wiser Christians. When facing a difficult battle, if you would just stop and search Scripture for guidance, ask a godly friend for advice, or even pray and ask God to help you approach the situation in a Christlike manner, you'd be surprised by how radically your perspective might shift. Those are simple, practical ways we can move our battle with the Enemy into the spiritual realm. When you do so, you experience the empowerment that God promises only to His brand ambassadors.

For instance, there are many people open to "spirituality." This openness has led many to seek alternative means of understanding themselves and life. They go to tarot-card readers. A few years ago, my wife went to a salon to get her hair done. The owners had expanded what they offered in the shop, and one of the things was a tarot-card reader you could consult while waiting for your hair appointment. That was my wife's last time there. She didn't sever the relationships she had made in the salon, but she refused to remain where the devil was given space.

When you represent God, you are to be locked in with His brand, not the Enemy's. Most brand ambassadors are under contract to wear only the brand they represent. They can wear items from noncompeting brands but can't wear a competitor's. They lose their deal if they wear another brand or refuse to wear in public the brand they're endorsing. God doesn't want us to wear the Enemy's products or act as though we aren't connected to His products. He wants us to joyously represent Him.

Being in urban ministry can be tough. My goal most of the time is to keep score like God does. What I mean is that I try not to allow success in the eyes of humans to trump what is successful in the eyes of the Most High. However, being in a challenging context, it is easy to fall into the trap of comparing the results of my ministry to the results of other ministries. I wonder why I am not seeing the same fruit as others, and this comparison mindset causes me to drift. If I am not careful, I will fall into the trap of elevating my personal preferences rather than submitting to

God's principles and purposes revealed in His Word. It's hard because some days I'm focused on living faithfully for God in my context, whereas other days I lose focus and start comparing. Because of that, I need people around who keep me on track about the mission God has given me. Accountability is one of God's gifts He uses to jolt me back to what He wants me to do.

This way of thinking isn't merely for people in full-time ministry; it's for all the saints. The Bible is full of stories of people in secular vocations leveraging their positions and assignments for God's kingdom. Joseph used his power, position, and vocation to preserve God's redeeming family—the sons of Israel and those who would lead to Jesus generations later. Esther used her power, position, and influence to aid the people of God. Nehemiah used his role and relationship in his marketplace to help rebuild the walls of Jerusalem. Daniel used his vocation in government to speak truth to power, not fearing for his job. In the Gospels, there are stories of women who worked in the marketplace and in other roles supporting Jesus's ministry. Acts tells us of Lydia, who continued to work in the fashion industry after trusting Christ. She allowed her home to be used for gospel ministry in the city (see Acts 16:14–15). Those stories should inspire vision in us for ministry we could be doing in the various contexts God has placed us. We all have our parts to play in the economy of God, no matter our human assignment. God uses people who are in power as well as those who are marginalized.

The black church in America is a star witness for the Lord despite the challenges she had to overcome to nurture black people, welcome all people, and be the conscience of a country that refused to let her people have equal footing:

> In keeping with its history, the African-American church remains at the forefront of urban ministry, binding the wounds of

injustice and seeking more just patterns of life. When virtually every other church left the city, the black church remained, its witness irrepressible.[7]

From the African Methodist Episcopal Church (AME) during slavery to the Baptist churches during the Jim Crow era to the multifaceted churches of today led by blacks, the black church has been living out its calling to be ambassadors for Christ. Thanks to the black church filling in the gaps for blacks during periods of slavery and segregation, there is an expectation for the black community to be witnesses to Christ in a way that no other religious or sociological group deals with.

Many in the Black Conscious Community often ask, "Why doesn't the black church show itself to be more active in other aspects of the community like it did in the past?" My answer is that the civil rights movement kept the black church from being the core artery of the black community as various other options that were closed to blacks were made open.

The process of secularization in black communities has always meant a diminishing of the influence of religion and an erosion in the central importance of black churches. . . . There is some evidence that the present and past central importance of the Black Church may be threatened by the virtual explosion of opportunities, which are now becoming available to recent black college graduates. An officially segregated society contributed to the dominant role black churches were able to maintain as one of the few cohesive black institutions to emerge from slavery. Talented black men and women developed their leadership skills in black churches and used them as launching pads for professional careers in the church or elsewhere in black society like education, music, and entertainment. With the breakdown of official segregation, some opportunities in previously closed professions in law, medicine, politics, and business have opened up as never before.[8]

In the past, black churches have helped start banks, credit unions, schools, historically black colleges, shelters, grocery stores, health clinics, and other institutions in the black community that gave constant common ground for the gospel. Other means of witnessing included Vacation Bible School, summer programs, bill relief, substance-abuse rehabilitation, prison aftercare, and scholarships to college. The black church took Titus 3:14 extremely seriously: "Let our people learn to devote themselves to good works for pressing needs, so that they will not be unfruitful." Today, the black church must continue to engage in good deeds to meet pressing needs so they will not be unfruitful.

The black church serves as the most profound witness of the gospel to this day. My point is that God empowers a seemingly powerless people group who knows and serves Jesus to do powerful things. That's Holy Spirit empowerment at its best.

Between 1982 and 1995, the seventeenth pastor of First African Baptist Church of Savannah, Reverend Thurmond Neill Tillman, consciously continued to combine the church's "spiritual or privatistic mission with its social or communal mission." Tillman, a former probation officer and apprentice aircraft pilot, emphasized the development of church-anchored programs for neighborhood youth, including juveniles who had gotten into trouble with the law. With 200 years of outreach tradition to guide him, Tillman explained the church's mission: "Whatever the needs of the people, that they cannot meet themselves, it is the mission of the church to help them. We can tackle any problem our people face because the church comes to the problem not bound by its own resources and capacities. The church is God's representative on earth. We have access to all the resources that implies."[9]

Churches such as the Greater Allen AME Cathedral in Queens still commit themselves to this type of profound ministry in their communities and beyond.

> Over the last decade, [Reverend Floyd H.] Flake's 8,000-member congregation has raised millions of dollars and devoted count-less volunteer hours to the slow, but steady redevelopment of the church's surrounding working-class Queens community. Equally impressive, in 1992 Flake launched the Shekinah Youth Chapel in Jamaica Queens, one of the city's poorest, most drug- and crime-torn minority neighborhoods.[10]

Many other churches from urban centers shine as examples of being healthy brand ambassadors.

WHERE DO WE GO FROM HERE?

One of the most challenging tasks of discipleship is getting the people you are training to see their roles as missionaries and to live as witnesses for Christ. All believers are called to be missionaries, not just overseas but wherever they are right now. Acts 2:47 tells us, "Every day the Lord added to their number those who were being saved." That wasn't merely when the apostles were preaching; it was as people were in their communities living and sharing their faith. Disciples were going house to house, sharing meals and un-doubtedly inviting their neighbors over, where they would hear the good news about Jesus (see verses 46–47). The implication in Acts 2 is that there was a healthy, Spirit-filled culture in the early church, exemplified by believers living in a giving, loving community with one another. The Spirit-filled community of the early church was really attractive to the watching world. The way believers were treating one another was countercultural. The way the saints conducted themselves wasn't normal, and the beauty of their relationship with one another blew away those who were around them. People didn't just hear the gospel; they saw it.

A little more than a decade ago, we had a partner church that had a member who owned a playground company. He wanted to give us a playground to have a safe place for kids in our community to play, as our church is in the trenches of North Philly and tons of violence and poverty surround us.

So, we had volunteers from the church work with the member's team to build it. While we were building it, people were walking past and asking what we were doing. We told them we were building a playground. They asked why, and we said we wanted a safe place for kids in our neighborhood to play. Some of our Muslim neighbors passed by and complimented us for being a blessing to the neighborhood. Now that the playground is built, day-care centers use it for recess during the warmer months. We are also able to use it for the after-school program and summer programs we run.

The time to rebrand the church to the world is now. We can't control when falsehoods come against us, but we *can* control our commitment to the gospel witness and do a better job of serving our cities.

That is why God has called and mobilized the church as a "rescue unit" to go out into the world and be His witnesses, turning people on their way to hell toward heaven. "You will be my witnesses," Jesus said (Acts 1:8). It is the local church's job to equip its members to go out among the dying and bring them a message of life. You are never further from the heart of God than you are when you are silent to your unsaved friends and loved ones about the gospel and the eternal life that Jesus gives. Telling others about Jesus and how they can be saved draws us closer to the heart of God.

You may be thinking, *I'm just an average church member. What can I do?* The truth is, you are far from average in God's eyes. You are a chosen ambassador, uniquely positioned in your workplace, neighborhood, and social circles to represent Jesus. Consider this: How can you live out the gospel in your daily life? Where could you volunteer at your church or in your community? Might you invite a neighbor over for a meal and genuine conversation? Perhaps you could use your professional skills to serve your church or community. Remember, the early church grew not just through the apostles' preaching but also through ordinary believers living extraordinary, Spirit-filled lives. You have the same Holy Spirit empowering you, so step out of your comfort zone. Be intentional about representing Christ in your sphere of influence. Whether it's through acts of kindness, speaking truth in love, or simply being present for those in need, you have the power to change perceptions and point people to Jesus. The time to rebrand the church is now, and it starts with each one of us. Will you accept the challenge to be a true brand ambassador for Christ in your everyday life?

3

REBRANDING CHURCH LEADERSHIP

RECENTLY, I READ ABOUT A CHURCH IN BROOKLYN THAT WAS robbed—specifically, the pastor and his wife. They were robbed of between half a million to a million dollars in jewelry. News of the incident went viral on TikTok, Instagram, Facebook, Snapchat, YouTube—everywhere. When I read the story, I hoped everybody was all right. Churches should be safe places, and we should do whatever we can to protect parishioners and pastors. But I was also confused. Maybe it's a new era, but I'm trying to wrap my mind around a pastor and his wife having in their possession, at church no less, half a million to a million dollars in jewelry. Now, on the one hand, they could have gotten the money to afford that jewelry from some entrepreneurial venture prior to pastoring or parallel to it. My issue, though, is this: Even if you can do it, should you? Why were they housing such expensive jewelry in their church building?

This same pastor, not long after that incident, showed off his prayer closet on social media, and it looked more like a boutique than a place of prayer. And if you think I am being judgmental, it should be noted that he was recently indicted on charges of fraud for coercing members of his church out of their retirement funds.[1]

My heart is broken because the level of distrust people feel for churches and church leaders today seems to be at an all-time high, and when pastors defraud their own congregations, we're often not surprised. With all the false teachers and prophets running rampant in the world and online, I'm disheartened by how many people are being deceived and misled. This chapter is for those who want to build up their discernment meter in understanding how to assess whether a leader or teacher is qualified for ministry. Also, it will speak to those who want to have a healthy assessment of who they follow.

When you see what's popular and place it next to Scripture, then share it with your circle and those online, you might seem extreme, overly critical, judgmental, and maybe even crazy. However, as you read this chapter, I hope you find a corner of remnant gospel community that doesn't stand for the madness.

This chapter is also for leaders—leaders who know better and are doing better; are committed to the Scriptures, their family, and Christ being formed in them; and are practically loving their city and stewarding their influence well.

And finally, I would be remiss not to say that this chapter is for those who may not yet realize that they are teaching false doctrine. It is my hope and prayer that this chapter serves as a wake-up call for those who are leading the body of Christ astray—that they would repent and take responsibility for the damage their false teaching has caused.

Many television shows portray black pastors and churches in scandalous ways. The pastor is a womanizer, a thief, or lacking considerable integrity. As I've peered into those stories and shows,

I'm grieved that some of these things are actually true. And I'm even more saddened that a healthier narrative rarely gets any play in the public eye. I'm not saying that comprehensively unhealthy churches don't exist, as there are plenty of them, but I rarely see the good ones go viral, particularly around church leadership. What follows are some characteristics that help us as believers begin the process of discernment on our journeys as parishioners and practitioners of the kingdom.

CHARACTER

When I was asked to consult with a historic black church, I met with their pulpit committee and my first question was, "What do you look for in a pastor?" They said, "We look for a good preacher and leader." I asked them, "Have you examined the biblical characteristics for eldership in the Bible?" They proceeded to tell me no. I then did a presentation on Ezekiel 34, 1 Timothy 3, 2 Timothy 2, Titus 1, and 1 Peter 5. As I began to talk, they said they'd never heard teaching on those passages. They admitted that they could have been saved so much heartache if they would have used the Scriptures as a guideline to pick leadership. In addition, I asked them whether they evaluated the marriages of the pastors they have hired in the past. For some people, this might seem like overkill, but when I used to assess church planters, we always had a session with the spouse to get a quick gauge of the couple's marital health. The members of this pulpit committee admitted they hadn't thought of that but realized it would be extremely prudent to add to their effort.

Gifts are easy to spot, but character can only be proven over time. That is why Paul starts with character when talking about what it means to be a pastor. Paul says pastors must be "above reproach" (1 Timothy 3:2), "meaning they should live in such a way that they should not be worthy of moral criticism."[2] This does not include false allegations but rather ones that can be founded.

When selecting a pastor, we have to be careful, as the more gifted a person in leadership tends to be, the more likely we will be to overlook character issues. That is why you need to have clear expectations regarding the kind of character you expect of the leaders in your church. If you are not clear on those things up front, you will relax or tweak character qualifications to fit certain people. Churches that compromise their standards to make way for talented pastors are likely enabling those pastors' bad behavior. Too often, extremely gifted people become the subject of major scandal. Henry and Richard Blackaby present some key insights into the issue of character in leadership in their landmark book on spiritual leadership:

> Christian organizations seem willing to overlook significant character flaws, and even moral lapses, as long as their leader continues to produce. . . .
>
> The characteristics God builds into spiritual leaders over time include wisdom, integrity, honesty, and moral purity. A proper relationship with God involves faith, obedience, and love for him. Although God often used people who appeared to be the least likely candidates for true leadership, the common denominator was these people had godly character, and they walked closely with him (1 Sam. 16:7). The larger God's assignment, the greater the character and the closer the relationship with God is required (Matt. 25:23).[3]

When Paul says that elders must be "above reproach," he doesn't mean they should be perfect; he means they should be mature, committed, and spiritually minded. The last thing our pulpits and ministries need are men and women who are child-ish. When Paul says, "Flee from youthful passions, and pursue righteousness, faith, love, and peace, along with those who call on the Lord from a pure heart" (2 Timothy 2:22), it is important to note that "most people think of 'youthful passions' as sex, but the phrase spans broader than that. It points to immaturity. Youth-ful means characterized by the traits, behavior, or other aspects of a younger person. *Passions*, plural, means a cornucopia of things that are inherent to those who haven't reached emotional, psy-chological, spiritual, and human maturity. This often includes lust: coveting, craving, and an unrestrained desire for something forbidden."[4]

Today, immaturity is often masqueraded as being real and au-thentic. It can be everything from unwholesome language to in-appropriate illustrations. Recently, I was listening to a preacher speak on an Instagram reel. The preacher ended up using slang terms for body parts and sex as an illustration for entering a de-monic portal. I was appalled! Especially in the pulpit, we have to use speech that reflects honor to God and dignity to people made in His image. More and more, the world is watching what the church is doing and how leaders are leading. Our posts, reels, videos, and actual lives give people a window into the life of the church. We shine light into the world, not add to the darkness or cause more confusion. Jesus states it plainly: "It would be better for him if a millstone were hung around his neck and he were thrown into the sea than for him to cause one of these little ones to stumble" (Luke 17:2). Our work should bring people closer to God, not escort them into darkness, confusion, falsehood, and unbelief. As Paul says, "We live in such a way that no one will stumble because of us, and no one will find fault with our minis-try" (2 Corinthians 6:3, NLT). At the end of the day, great leaders have a heart for the glory of God to be seen and for their role to contribute to people seeing it and knowing Jesus.

People shouldn't be unsure about our standards for Christian leadership. I long for the day when the words *pastor* and *Christian leader* come with automatic respect and dignity—a day when people have encountered so many men and women being solid disciples and healthy humans that Christian leadership is rebranded.

COMPETENCY

I once heard the late Dr. A. Lewis Patterson Jr. say, "A call to ministry is a call to preparation." We live in a day when ignorance is celebrated. Recently, a prominent preacher said we don't need theology. He suggested that theology boxes God in, not knowing that his atheology was a theology in itself. We also live in a world where people think they can become experts at something by watching a five-minute video or ninety-second reel. I believe there needs to be some level of educational and discipleship standards for those coming into church leadership. I don't mean that everyone has to have a seminary degree, but there should be a level of standardized education and testing to know if leaders who will be teaching the Bible have a handle on the biblical text and sound doctrine.

As a parishioner, you must have a level of biblical literacy in order to have an educated ear. In the early stages of my walk as a believer, this was very helpful. I was a twenty-year-old college student new to the faith. My friends and I would spend tons of time in the Word. Even as new, immature Christians, we saw the difference between truth and error early. (And this was well before the internet and social media.) Through the Holy Spirit, you are innately equipped by God with discernment. Use it. Study the Bible and ask God to help you discern truth from error.

COMMITMENT

One Sunday when our church was still a relatively young church plant, we were transitioning off receiving financial support from other churches, organizations, and individuals. Leading up to this, I was frustrated because I was spending enormous amounts of time raising money from outside Epiphany Fellowship to serve our church and our city. Because of that, in my Sunday sermon, I quoted from 2 Corinthians 11:8: "I robbed other churches by taking pay from them to minister to you." Paul taught a sacrifice in ministry that should be apparent. Most solid leaders I know would lead God's people for free. That's commitment. Paul was so committed to reaching the Corinthians that when he first came to them, he avoided talking about money. It's not that he couldn't receive money. Paul's point here isn't to guilt the Corinthians but to let them know his heart for them and Christ. In addition, he sought to contrast himself with those who were coming in to take advantage of the Corinthians. He was doing something counter-cultural to how they lived. "Paul *embraces* low status: he became the Corinthians' servant."[5] Notice the difference: "False apostles demanded money, whereas Paul moved differently when on gospel mission. The 'super apostles' obviously expected to be paid (see 2:17). Apparently, they had suggested to the Corinthians that it was a sign of Paul's inferiority that he declined financial support."[6] According to the Bible, commitment isn't just about *how much* you labor; it's about *how* you labor.

CHURCH-LEADER COMPETENCIES

Every follower of Jesus, from the new believer to the seasoned veteran Christian, needs to understand the role of pastors. While it might seem obvious, I think it's easy to make assumptions about what pastors are *supposed* to do without actually going to our ultimate source of truth for how the church should operate: the Scripture. So let's answer two very simple questions about pastors:

1. What are pastors called to do in the church?
2. How does that relate to you?

Much can be solved by understanding expectations. Pastoral leadership is defined by God, not us. His people should have clear categories of what shepherds are supposed to be doing. That helps all parties to avoid creating expectations that aren't in the Bible. Understanding the role of a pastor can help you find a good church home. And while I would be very careful about encouraging anyone to leave their church, knowing the role of a pastor might help you discern whether it is time to make a change. Churches where pastors are not functioning within their biblical role are rarely healthy.

Based on Acts 15, Titus 1:5, and 1 Timothy 4:14, there should be a community of shepherds in every church with a pastor who operates as a first among equals—one who acts as a rudder or visionary or communicator for the whole. With that in mind, the following characteristics would be embodied by the whole pastoral team and not just rest on one shepherd. Each leader will practice their role in differing and varying capacities but should meet God's design and requirements for that role.

Pastor, bishop, and *elder* are interchangeable terms for the same office. When we read the following passages about pastors, we get a sense of their role within the church:

- **1 Peter 5:1–4.** Pastors should . . .
  o Care for and stay connected to the flock
  o Feed the flock (see also Ezekiel 34; Malachi 2:7)

- **1 Timothy 5:17–21; Titus 1:5–9.** Pastors are to . . .
  o Lead the church, exercising authority wisely by watching over the church
  o Cast vision for the church
  o Protect the church from false teaching

- **1 Timothy 4:14.** Pastors should operate in . . .
  o A community of equals, or "council of elders"
  o Mutual accountability and consensus

I know that many church traditions have differing leadership structures, but the above is where I land based on what I see in Scripture. Let's take a closer look at the pastors' duties in the local church and why they matter to you.

Lead

Paul states, "The elders who are good leaders are to be considered worthy of double honor, especially those who work hard at preaching and teaching" (1 Timothy 5:17). The word *leaders* refers to those who rule, guide, and direct. In order to lead, leaders need to understand what God wants for His flock and guide the sheep in that direction. That looks like a practical vision that is rooted in Scripture and sensitive to context. People need to be clear on what God's goals are for the church and what that practically looks like *where* you are doing ministry. In other words, context matters. Let me explain.

In a suburban church, the outreach might look different from that of an urban church. Mega, medium, and micro church outreaches will function differently because of not just context but also cultural currency. For example, my church is in a transient, inner-city context, so we started an after-school program to help address our community's low literacy rates. We also did a boxing league with three hundred youth and young adults. The league was designed to help with the anger and mental health challenges in the inner city, and we staffed people from the city to help. We also organized a basketball league because several of the schools around us lost funding for sports programs; we stepped up to serve our community and meet a clear felt need. By contrast, however, I went to speak at a megachurch in a suburb in the Midwest years ago. Their men's outreach had monster trucks, the Spider-Man movie's stunt double doing tricks, thousands of pounds of BBQ, and much more. It was one of the most over-the-top yet creative outreach endeavors I've seen. It would not work in my context, but it seemed to work in theirs.

For discipleship, some churches have Sunday school, small groups, Wednesday Bible study, or men's and women's ministry. Some churches have all of the above. Discipleship isn't limited to those forms of engagement. There are also organic means that promote a more life-on-life approach. My point is that the leader must be clear on how they are going to facilitate Christ being formed in people. Leaders must have the acumen to lead their church clearly.

The Bible teaches, "Where there is no vision, the people are unrestrained, but happy is he who keeps the law" (Proverbs 29:18, NASB). *Vision* here means to see God's truth and guide people toward it. In essence, it means to guide God's people in His direction. Our leading of the people must be a direct reflection of Jesus's leading of us. Jesus was clear with us about who He is, why He came to dwell among us, and what He came to accomplish (see Matthew 28:18–20; Acts 1:8). The Sermon on the Mount and the upper-room discourse are examples of how Jesus casts vision for His followers.

In any effective rebranding effort, leadership is one of the most important components. Do those who are given charge of

God's people lead them in His way? That is the difference between a false leader and a true one. If you are a pastor, determine right now to submit your leadership to the authority of Scripture and cast a vision for your church. Once a year at my church, we have a Vision Sunday where I report on the ministries of our church over the past year and cast a vision of where we want to go and how our membership can help. If you are a member of a church and not in leadership, know that you can ask for clarity and vision. Let the pastors and elders of your church know that you want to be led—that you want them to cast vision on how you can help point people to Jesus in your particular context.

You should know where your church is going. You should even request (if the pastor hasn't offered it) a written copy of the vision and mission statements of the church. Also, ask how the church intends to strategically live out that vision. You might even inquire about the strategic steps and timelines for the pastor's goals. It would be helpful to suggest that leaders have a Vision Sunday once or twice a year. In addition, ask your leaders how you can help support the vision and mission of the church. Ask how you can be praying for the vision of the church to come to fruition. Ask where you can serve. That will help you and others have a deeper connection to the mission of God in your local assembly.

Feed

Ezekiel 34 warns the shepherds of Israel about their role in the spiritual anemia of the sheep: "Son of man, prophesy against the shepherds of Israel. Prophesy, and say to them, 'This is what the Lord GOD says to the shepherds: Woe to the shepherds of Israel, who have been feeding themselves! Shouldn't the shepherds feed their flock?" (verse 2). "The people as a flock were given in trust, and eventually the king was called to account for his exercise of the office of shepherd. The judgment against the shepherds of Israel in Ezekiel 34 indicates that Israelite kings often came up short in meeting the demands of their divine commissioning as shepherds of their people."[7] Priests and prophets were also included in the category of "shepherd." And we must always remember that the primary function of a shepherd is to care for their sheep.

When Jesus restored Peter after Peter denied Jesus three times, Jesus asked him,

> "Simon, son of John, do you love me more than these?"
> "Yes, Lord," he said to him, "you know that I love you."
> "Feed my lambs," he told him. A second time he asked him,
>   "Simon, son of John, do you love me?"
> "Yes, Lord," he said to him, "you know that I love you."
> "Shepherd my sheep," he told him.
> He asked him the third time, "Simon, son of John, do you
>   love me?"
> Peter was grieved that he asked him the third time, "Do you
>   love me?" He said, "Lord, you know everything; you
>   know that I love you."
> "Feed my sheep," Jesus said. (John 21:15–17)

Over and over again, Jesus stressed to Peter as a leader, "If you love Me, then feed My sheep." In other words, a loving shepherd makes it a priority to nourish the sheep. And the best way to nourish the flock is with God's Word (see 1 Peter 2:2).

I was taught that the body needs a balanced diet. In the same way, you need to preach and teach through books, doctrine, theology, topical exposition, felt needs, and current issues. Today, many pastors do either one-offs or topical sermons. There's nothing wrong with topical sermons, but many of them are more motivational and individualistic in orientation than sermons that focus on a particular passage. A key in preaching and teaching is that our feeding must come from Scripture and be supported by the verses surrounding the text; in other words, context matters. Because of the amount of misinformation out there about the Christian faith, Jesus, and the church, we can't afford to be faulty feeders of the people of God. We have to be skilled in taking God's people from milk to meat (see Hebrews 5:11–6:2).

I ask you this: Do you have the auditory endurance to hear more than felt needs? Are you hungry enough to want multidimensional meals? I also know churches where pastors preach only book studies of the Bible. I don't think that's a balanced diet, although I know you can cover books in an engaging way. Other churches do only topical sermon series on things like purpose, money, relationships. That is not a balanced diet either. The Bible says that people won't endure what is sound but will accumulate for themselves teachers to suit their own passions (see 2 Timothy 4:3).

Here's a quick tip for anyone looking for a church home: What if you learned to find teachers who are in sync with God's desires? Reverse narcissism, if you will. With all the technology out there, you should be able to go online and survey a church's diet. Just like when you go to the store and look at the nutritional information on the back of a cereal box, you should survey the diet of teaching you might be getting at a particular church before visiting.

If you are not in church leadership, I would encourage you to communicate with the leaders about what you see as your generation's perceived and communicated needs. If you are in a ministry where the pastor isn't clear on what's going on in today's society, it'd be great if you sent them podcasts, shows, documentaries, and maybe articles to keep them informed so that they can shepherd the flock well. My folks send me pods with crazy world-views that are shepherding and shaping the next generation. I love it because they help me feed them better. They help me see and understand some of the false messages that are gaining traction, and then I can better equip my church to hold fast to the truth of the gospel.

Care

When everything shut down in 2020, we hoped the pandemic would be a short spell and we'd bounce back quickly. However, we soon found out that season would be much longer than expected. As time went on, my leaders and I split up the church membership list and started making calls. We asked our people what they needed, how they were, and how we could better connect. Our desire was to find practical ways to care for the flock.

Care is one of the key components of shepherding in the Bible. In fact, Scripture refers to God as our shepherd: "The LORD is my shepherd, I lack nothing. He takes me to lush pastures" (Psalm 23:1–2, NET). David begins Psalm 23 by speaking about God's active care for those who belong to Him. Having been a shepherd to sheep and a shepherd of Israel, David never forgot that even in that role, *he* is one of God's sheep too.

In today's church, there seems to be an outcry for care. No matter what I post online about church leadership and the state of the church, one of the most frequently evoked issues is church hurt, which is a care issue. Author and pastor Jerome Gay defines it this way: "Church hurt is a form of spiritual malpractice that happens when Christians deviate from the standards of love and care laid out in Scripture and cause harm to Christ's body."[8] There is intentional and unintentional church hurt. Both need to be examined and addressed, particularly with seeking peace. Yahweh doesn't mince words when He deals with abuse issues in the church. Scripture is clear: "If possible, as far as it depends on you, live at peace with everyone" (Romans 12:18). Making things right with people is an important part of leading and caring.

One time during a sermon, I shared an illustration of a Chinese person. I didn't feel that it was offensive, and everyone laughed it off. After the service, a young Chinese American woman asked to speak to me in my office with her husband. She said, "I just hate that this was the first time I heard you speak of a Chinese person, and it was negative." While I initially wanted to defend myself, I chose to step back and listen. I sought to empathize with her. I apologized profusely and publicly. Another time I preached a message on race and received a thoughtfully critical email from a faithful and wise couple in my church. The next Sunday, I issued a public apology from the pulpit and across all social media platforms. The conviction from the Holy Spirit I felt from the email and 2 Corinthians 6:3 arrested me. After doing this, many people expressed that the apology itself brought healing.

It is important to me to recognize that I possess power as a leader and, as a result, can manipulate situations where I am wrong. If I am not careful, I will make others the culprit by controlling the narrative with my position and power. In response to this temptation, I think our churches need a resurgence of care. Care goes such a long way toward helping the people in our churches grow and flourish. If you are a church leader, recognize your power and wield it carefully and with humility. If you are a church member, consider how you might participate in promoting a culture of care in your faith community.

We had a church member lose someone in their family, and they didn't have the funds to pay for the funeral, so the church took on the bill. That act gave us cred with the family. In another instance, we had a non-member lose all her limbs, and her family was unable to pay to have their home made handicap accessible for her to function. We paid a significant amount as a church to help her.

I think we need to be careful not to place all the burden of care on pastors; every member of the church is called to participate actively in the ministry of care. I do believe, however, that pastors can and should use their influence and teaching to foster a culture of care in their churches.

We need to communicate to our churches what care looks like and what methods and means are available, such as benevolence, pastoral care, and crisis intervention. If you are a leader, survey your people for some of the most common needs within your church and in the surrounding community. However, the "one another" commands in the Bible let us know that the body has to play a role as well. Involve church members in brainstorming needs and developing systems of care. You might even consider making this part of your small-group ministry. Recently, one of our church's leaders had a major house fire and lost everything. We have a decent budget set aside for relief care in the church. It was amazing to help this pastor out until the insurance kicked in. But what was most amazing was the outpouring that came from the church on how to help. When that happened, we were able to quickly create a needs analysis, and people began pouring out their love through very practical means, including clothes, babysitting, and monetary gifts. "Carry one another's burdens; in this way you will fulfill the law of Christ" (Galatians 6:2).

It is important that you give thought to how you will care for people's needs. Burden-bearing systems must be well thought-out as new issues come up, such as autistic children needing development programs, people in wheelchairs needing accessibility, and even older saints needing their front sidewalks shoveled in the winter. These are examples of the church being the church and are powerful means of pointing people to Jesus.

Know

An important aspect of leadership that bleeds into every area of ministry is knowing the sheep. Knowing people well allows the leader to contextualize and customize their leading, feeding, caring, and protecting in their particular sector of the vineyard. Because my church is made up of mostly millennials and Gen Z and only some Gen X and boomers, I tweak my exegesis to their experiences. The Bible says, "Know well the condition of your flock, and pay attention to your herds" (Proverbs 27:23). The word for know is an interesting word in the Hebrew. The word is *yāda*, and it is used for "the most intimate acquaintance."[9] The idea is to know something on a deep level.

I've had to realize that my people might be being guided by aspects of culture from *The Breakfast Club*, Joe Budden, *FreshandFit*, Aba N Preach, Anton Daniels, *Drink Champs*, *The Brilliant Idiots*, *Million Dollaz Worth of Game*, Tasha K, and more. A quick survey of those outlets gives me a bird's-eye view into what is happening all around them. Parishioners need to assist the pastor in knowing them and what they are dealing with. I love interacting with my folks on social media. They send me things that help me know how to minister to them, whether they are posts on mental health, theological questions, apologetics, or relationship issues. I often respond by posting reels (with their permission) on social media. I have found that it helps people get direction on important issues as well as discern truth from error.

On another note, small groups are also windows through which to get to know people in your church. Our small-group leaders help me and the other elders know what's going on with people and what needs members have that might require a larger system developed to facilitate growth. For instance, there is only so much financial help a single small group can provide. Therefore, we developed a benevolence ministry to help with more extensive issues—ongoing health concerns, large unexpected medical bills, and so on.

Protect

When I was in seminary, I wrote a paper on false teachers. As I began my study, I realized that a significant amount of the New Testament speaks about false teachers. The writers speak of protecting the church from within and without. There were external forces that came against the church, and those who paraded themselves as sent by God were actually wolves in sheep's clothing. We are dealing with an unprecedented number of attacks on the church. Members also have to be part of making sure the church is protected. Paul talks about the role all believers should and must engage in to protect the church: "I urge you, brothers and sisters, to watch out for those who create divisions and obstacles contrary to the teaching that you learned. Avoid them" (Romans 16:17). Gossip and slander must be shut down. That doesn't mean we should ignore things that do need to be addressed, but the challenge is to make sure that falsehood doesn't get the oxygen to grow.

Peter spends an entire chapter on the topic, as in this verse: "There were indeed false prophets among the people, just as there will be false teachers among you. They will bring in destructive heresies, even denying the Master who bought them, and will bring swift destruction on themselves" (2 Peter 2:1).

Paul told Timothy that one of his primary reasons for leaving him in Ephesus was to protect the church: "As I urged you when I went to Macedonia, remain in Ephesus so that you may instruct certain people not to teach false doctrine" (1 Timothy 1:3). He even names people: "Among them are Hymenaeus and Alexander, whom I have delivered to Satan, so that they may be taught not to blaspheme" (verse 20).

Titus was left in Crete by Paul to get the churches in order, and one of the areas required for order was protection: "There are many rebellious people, full of empty talk and deception, especially those from the circumcision party. It is necessary to silence them; they are ruining entire households by teaching what they shouldn't in order to get money dishonestly" (Titus 1:10–11).

My favorite passage on a shepherd's protection in the Bible is "Your rod and your staff—they comfort me" (Psalm 23:4). John Walton points out that "the 'rod' was a clublike weapon used to defend a flock against predators; the same word is used for a royal 'scepter.' . . . The 'staff' could also serve as a weapon, but it was used to prod sheep in the right direction—hence a metaphor of divine guidance."[10] I see it as my role to direct and guide our church as we submit to Jesus.

Years ago, there was a guy who was manipulating women in our church and sleeping with them. We were a young church at the time, and it came to my attention what he was doing. I stepped in and challenged him, and we placed him under a discipline process for restoration. Instead of submitting to the process, he (while going through a divorce) began dating a young lady and lied about it. Prior to this, many of us told the woman it was a bad idea. Because this man would not take responsibility for his predatory behavior, we had to remove him from membership, but she decided to accept his engagement. They are now divorced. Leaders have to protect the church even though many times the people don't understand why they're being disciplined. They are similar to my kids: They may at times want to do something, but I say no, and they view my protection as a harsh restriction, not knowing they are in grave danger.

In another instance, a young man was sowing false doctrine in the church. He had the conspiracy-theorist bug, and I didn't find fault with it initially. I loved and entertained his questions no matter how off-the-wall their content was. He had deep friend-ships in the church, and I invested a lot in him and his sweet wife. I conducted their premarital counseling, presided over their wedding, and dedicated their kids. I even hired him for a few projects. As time went on, he began to delve deep into some con-cerning false doctrines and spread them. After giving him several warnings, we had to remove him from church membership.

One of the hardest things as a shepherd in defending the flock is protecting people who don't know they are in danger—people who don't feel they need protecting. In fact, some of them believe that your protection is control and spiritual abuse, and they would trust a wolf more than you.

Parishioners must participate in protecting the congrega-tion. When the shepherds raise issues, there needs to be coop-eration from those in the flock. Because of the relationship that people may have with those the leaders are trying to protect them from, they tend to minimize or downplay the potential dangers of division. Sometimes it takes time to see, but when the flock finally understands, they often help protect the church and might even assist in guiding the challenging individuals toward repentance.

A church is at its greatest health when its members and lead-ers are on the same page as God and one another. It takes time for that to happen. Leaders must create ways for the congregation to encourage and have healthy critique. Believers must respectfully communicate with leaders. Both "should be quick to listen, slow to speak, and slow to anger" (James 1:19). When concerns come up, they must not be demonized but instead given humble con-sideration, particularly if they are valid and many other people affirm the same thing.

CONCLUSION

All in all, rebranding church leadership is a work of God through leaders and parishioners. Both groups have to be committed to God's glory and being salt and light. Just like in Acts 6 and 15, the church is healthiest when sheep and shepherds alike are committed to church health.

4

REBRANDING DISCIPLESHIP

THE CHURCH HAS THE BEST PRODUCT THE WORLD COULD EVER ASK for: the gospel of Jesus Christ. However, too often we have the most chaotic, unclear philosophy and practice of discipleship. We know we need to grow to be like Christ, but no one seems to be on the same page about how to get there. Everyone—both the leaders and the people in the pews—has different expectations regarding spiritual growth.

> In the New Testament salvation and discipleship are so closely related as to be indivisible. They are not identical, but as with Siamese twins they are joined by a tie which can be severed only at the price of death.[1]

I went into a Wingstop restaurant during the pandemic. After ordering my food, I left to run a quick errand. When I came back to pick up my meal, I noticed that the manager was cursing at his disorganized and flustered staff. My order ended up being wrong, and the manager started yelling about it. His staff was supremely embarrassed, and I was embarrassed for them. As I watched, I noticed the way the fryers, preppers, saucers, baggers, and cashiers were not clear about their roles and places. It seemed they hadn't been well trained on how to work together. As problems came up, the manager began randomly calling workers to fix the problem, which escalated the mayhem. In addition, the store had filled with delivery drivers, more people waiting on mobile orders, and new customers hoping to order at the counter. The manager's only solution was to yell and curse. I suspect this Wingstop lost several customers that day, and it wasn't because of the wait. All of us customers waiting for our food could see what the manager was blind to: It was a leadership issue. The manager's team was struggling to keep up with demand because they weren't well developed and trained to handle the stressors they were facing. It wasn't a brand problem. They had a good product. It was a house problem—a leadership problem.

Any church can have a vision statement, a flashy website, and massive screens in the sanctuary. Your church might have the prettiest brochures, the most baptisms, the best Instagram page, the funniest clips, and the most entertaining stuff on TikTok but still be missing the mark. You can have all these beautiful things, but at the end of the day, if people are not growing and being conformed to the image of Christ, you have a problem. The Holy Spirit has a central goal for every believer: to make each one more like Jesus (see Romans 8:29). The Spirit's goal is to be the conductor of sanctification and spiritual growth. Discipleship is the means by which that goal is accomplished. It is our participation in the goal that matters, in both helping others look more like Jesus and holding ourselves responsible for being Christlike ourselves.

WHAT IS A DISCIPLE?

The church I grew up in had an altar call at the end of every Sunday service, complete with the deacons up front with their hands outstretched. That part of the service was referred to as the call to discipleship. In other words, becoming a Christian meant being a disciple. There are not fundamentally different species of Christians like there are for animals and plant life. Every disciple is a Christian, and every Christian is a disciple. My definition is this: "A disciple of Jesus Christ is one who has renounced themselves and pledged their life to being in a lifetime apprenticeship to the Lord Jesus Christ" (see Matthew 10:39). My goal as a disciple maker is to work myself out of a job with people. That is why sometimes in the process, I don't answer their questions; I point them to resources. I want the people I disciple to go find the answers themselves in Scripture. Jesus discipled the Twelve for three years intensively, then ascended to heaven and sent the Spirit (see Acts 1:8–11; 2:1–4). In essence, although His presence was with them through the Spirit, they had to be personally discerning and use what He had taught them over those three years.

John addressed the topic of discipleship a lot in his gospel. He often used the word *followed*. The word for *followed* shows up in the New Testament 89 times, and the word *disciple* shows up 261 times, which lets us know how important those terms are to our identity and function as believers. John initially used *followed* in the first chapter of his gospel: "The two disciples heard him say this and *followed* Jesus" (verse 37). That verse refers to two disciples of John the Baptist. When they heard John say, "Look, the Lamb of God" (verses 29, 36), they transitioned from following John to following Jesus from that day forward. Disciple makers are to push people toward Jesus and not themselves. *Followed* is a code word for being discipled, and it "is in the tense appropriate for once-for-all action, which may indicate that they cast in their lot with Jesus."[2] There must be a point where we decide we are committing our lives fully to the Master. To follow Jesus is to cast our lot with Him. That means orienting our lives around Him— obeying Him first and foremost. It means giving Him reign over more and more of who we are, how we see ourselves, and how we live.

THE STATE OF DISCIPLE MAKING IN THE CHURCH

In the church today, you rarely hear talk about being a disciple. We hear about purpose, season, the bag (money), relationships, or a come-up. I preach at several large and small events, and people often come up to me afterward saying that they rarely hear the word *disciple* and don't often hear teaching on how disciples must function. Being a disciple is fundamental to our faith. Everything in our lives flows from that designation; it is the ultimate identity of the Christian. Yet churches today seem focused on events. We have preaching fests, merch lines, and prophetic summits but offer little in the way of building people into healthy Christ followers. It seems we have wrongly associated discipleship with attending events rather than actively seeking and imitating Jesus. Discipleship cannot be relegated to an event or a resource; we must understand that it encompasses all of life. Being made into a disciple can include events, but it must not be reduced to any one mechanism.

Major Obstacles to Disciple Making

Unhealthy individuality is one of the most telling issues that affects our ability to grow. The Bible says, "One who isolates himself pursues selfish desires; he rebels against all sound wisdom" (Proverbs 18:1). In other words, people who isolate themselves are not merely unsociable; they are problems for society since they will defy sound judgment. The Mishnah, an ancient collection of Jewish oral tradition, "uses this proverb to teach the necessity of being part of a community because people have social responsibilities and need one another."[3] The Enemy prowls for those who break away from the flock. We are called sheep because we are a flock under the guidance of the Great Shepherd.

The relativism prevalent in the world today is making its way into the church. Now we are using the "my truth/your truth" paradigm. "*Relativism* is the belief that there's no absolute truth, only the truths that a particular individual or culture happen to believe. If you believe in *relativism*, then you think different people can have different views about what's moral and immoral."[4] There is no *my* truth and *your* truth; there is only *Jesus* the truth.

People want spiritual *advisors* rather than spiritual *authority*. Being an advisor doesn't always include accountability. It also doesn't promote imperatives. Advisors present options but possess little authority. If you want to grow in Christ, you need to invite spiritual authority into your life, which means inviting others in gospel community into your life for the purpose of influencing you. That doesn't mean we let others control us, but what it does mean is that others are given the freedom to encourage you and check you, and they must have a degree of leverage in your life.

I have peers and spiritual leaders whom my wife can call if I lose my mind. As a pastor, it is crucial that I not become an authoritative island unto myself. I need accountability, advice, and guidance, and I need to actively maintain an openness to these things. Jesus sets the way, not us. Whether it is because of bad experiences with the church or just plain rebellion, people want to write their own discipleship syllabi. People want to define their processes. No teacher lets students determine what's good for them or what they need in order to succeed. Seeker-sensitive churches do that, and it hinders the making of disciples.

Many times, as a means to hook people, churches conduct surveys to see what they want at church. There's nothing wrong with surveys. We should know what people's needs are and, at times, their wants. However, the cupcake sermons we often hear in this era, which lack nutritional value, are the result of that movement. "A seeker is an unbeliever that is outside the church but still searching (or 'seeking') for meaning and significance. Classic 'seeker sensitive' churches had a consumeristic mindset and were focused on the 'felt needs' of the lost people around them—especially people in suburban or affluent areas."[5] There isn't anything wrong with creating an attractional atmosphere in the church, but we must make sure that when someone is called to commit, they don't feel fooled by faulty advertising. We need to call people to follow Jesus and live for the glory of God and not just make people feel better about themselves.

The church is no longer expected to be central to spiritual formation. Many people feel they got along fine without going to church during the pandemic. The number of post-pandemic content creators and podcasts has gone through the roof. People are eating off multiple tables.

Spiritual abuse in the church has made many people rightly cautious about discipleship and communal connectivity. "What is spiritual abuse? Any attempt to exert power and control over someone using religion, faith, or beliefs can be spiritual abuse. Spiritual abuse can happen within a religious organization or a personal relationship."[6] Recently, several pastors have been called out publicly for acts of spiritual abuse. Oftentimes, hurt people cannot tell the difference between healthy engagement and control, and because controlling leaders are said to be rampant, people can sometimes become gun-shy of discipleship. I've had people court the church for years before becoming members. I then find out through the membership process or later about some of their past challenges with the church and why it took so long for them to lock into a community. On a side note, if you have recently experienced church hurt, you may need to set aside some time to heal—set aside a few months to just attend church without feeling the pressure to serve or lead in a particular ministry. I would encourage you to talk to a church leader you trust. Let them know you are hurting and need to devote the next season to healing.

People who have experienced and healed from church hurt have become some of the most helpful people in our church's ministry post-pandemic. For instance, in church business meetings, when it is time for questions, many ask questions out of their hurt over bad experiences with financial mismanagement or abuse of power. Others who have worked through that pain can help affirm those who are hurting and provide new perspective. The fact that we were having a meeting openly discussing finances and accountability was a culture shift for them; it was an example of the church being healthy in a way they'd never experienced before. That kind of transparency immediately settles the souls of those pained by ministries that have done the opposite.

REDUCTIONIST UNDERSTANDING OF DISCIPLESHIP

If we aren't careful, we will reduce discipleship to only one of its forms. One of the preferred forms people want is one-on-one discipleship. I remember members of one group saying to me, "Pastor, if you don't spend individual time with one person, you haven't discipled them." And I always tell people, "Show me where one-on-one discipleship is presented as the primary model of discipleship in the Bible. You won't find it." Most discipleship in the

Bible is communal. Reducing discipleship to a particular method-
ology lessens the amount of attention we pay to how comprehensive following Jesus actually is. Don't assume that if the church
isn't doing your preferred mechanism of discipleship, it isn't
doing discipleship. Don't assume your preferred method is the
only means of discipleship, and don't assume a one-on-one discipleship relationship is sufficient for growing in Christlikeness.
People will ask, "What about Elijah and Elisha, Paul and Timothy?"
These examples were born out of the context of community. For
example, when Paul picked up Timothy in Acts 16, he immediately placed him with Silas and others. Even Jesus didn't really do
individual discipleship. He did community discipleship: five hundred people, then twelve, and then three. He had layers, but one-
on-one was not His primary mode of discipleship.

In other churches, discipleship is reduced to whatever the
church is already doing: Sunday morning services, outreach events,
community-building activities, small groups, and so on. I would
submit to you, however, that programming does not equal discipleship. While any of those things *can* contribute to discipleship, we
shouldn't assume they do. If you are a church leader, take a moment to stop and consider whether the programs your church offers are actually helping people meet Jesus and grow to be more
like Him. If you are simply attending a church and not in leadership, ask yourself, *Are the events and programs I attend at church moving me*
closer to Jesus? Is my involvement in church helping me grow to be more like Jesus
and point other people to Him? It is easy to confuse activity with spiritual
growth. Just because you are doing lots of things doesn't mean
those things are the best use of your time and energy. Rebranding
the church might involve taking a long, hard look at the church
calendar with the goal of carefully considering what is actually
helping us accomplish our mission.

GETTING THE FUNDAMENTALS

The State of Theology conducted a poll about different areas of believers' basic understanding of the faith.[7] The poll asked, "Does God change?" Fifty-one percent of professing Christians polled said yes! Another question was "Does church membership matter?" Fifty-six percent said no! This one was the most telling of all: Forty-three percent of respondents said Jesus was a great teacher but wasn't God. Those statistics paint a dire picture of the state of spiritual formation in the church today.

I am deeply concerned by the lack of understanding of the fundamentals by most Christians. Even after having been in the faith for quite some time, many don't know the basics. That is why American churches are a mission field for cults and alternative ideologies. Many black mystery cults, such as Black Hebrew Israelites, prey on unassuming Christians and hijack them from the faith. Understanding our faith is paramount—not just for the sake of defending it, but because God wants us to make it a priority. It is not just leaders who need to know what they believe and why; we all do. That is why Peter says, "In your hearts regard Christ the Lord as holy, ready at any time to give a defense to anyone who asks you for a reason for the hope that is in you" (1 Peter 3:15). Peter is envisioning someone giving "a legal defense before a court."[8] Similarly, the writer of Hebrews challenges believers about their lack of spiritual growth (see 5:11–14). In 6:1–2, he explains some of those fundamentals. It can be translated "basic principles."[9]

When it comes to fundamentals, nothing is more important than what we believe about Jesus: who He is and what He has accomplished. Theologians call this Christology, the study of the person and work of Jesus Christ. If you feel hazy or uncertain about the fundamentals of your faith, start with who Jesus is and what He came to earth to do.

There are some other "ologies" that it would be helpful to familiarize yourself with. Hamartiology is the study of sin. Soteriology is the study of salvation. Ecclesiology is the study of the church. Theology is the study of God. Bibliology is the study of the formation, inerrancy, and infallibility of Scripture. The church needs to have these not only as classes but also weaved into expositional preaching, ministry development, leadership development, and outreach. We also must show the practical implications of these disciplines. Books like J. I. Packer's *Knowing God* and Jen Wilkin and J. T. English's *You Are a Theologian* are good places to start if you want to grow in your understanding of the essentials of the faith.[10] For those who want to dig even deeper, resources like *The Moody Handbook of Theology*, Wayne Grudem's *Systematic Theology*, and Charles Ryrie's *Basic Theology* offer plenty of valuable information.[11]

Knowledge alone doesn't grow people, as disciple making must be comprehensive. We will see later the different dimensions of discipleship. Author John Mark Comer talks about the limitations of knowledge alone: "A lot of churches operate on the assumption that as a person's knowledge of the Bible increases, their maturity will increase with it. I have been around Bible-teaching churches for my entire life, and I can assure you this is, at best, wildly insufficient."[12] In light of this, knowledge must be accompanied by other life-on-life aspects of spiritual formation, as we will see later.

In essence, the fundamentals help us develop a Christian worldview. A Christian worldview serves as a framework for those who know Jesus Christ, guiding them to develop their perspectives, interactions, and understanding of God, people, life, and decision-making based on the Bible (see 1 Corinthians 2:14–16).

A Christian worldview is at the bedrock of being a disciple. We are to think Christianly and act Christianly. That is why the fundamentals are enormously vital. These, coupled with spiritual disciplines, play vital roles in our looking more like Jesus Christ.

SPIRITUAL DISCIPLINES

Simply put, spiritual disciplines are God-ordained tools that help grow our intimacy with God, our souls in Him, and our output for Him. Spiritual disciplines are practices found in Scripture that promote spiritual growth among believers in the gospel of Jesus Christ. These habits of devotion and experiential Christianity have been practiced by the people of God since biblical times.[13] Author Donald Whitney categorizes two types: personal disciplines and interpersonal disciplines. Both play crucial roles in discipleship. Many times, when we think of spiritual disciplines, we think of what we do alone. But most disciplines have a communal aspect.

> Christians should read and study the Word of God on their own (personal Spiritual Disciplines), but they should also hear the Bible read and study it with the church (interpersonal Spiritual Disciplines). Christians should worship God privately, but they should also worship Him publicly with His people. Some Spiritual Disciplines are by nature practiced alone, such as journaling, solitude, and fasting (though individuals sometimes fast in conjunction with a congregational fast). Other Disciplines are by nature congregational, such as fellowship.[14]

Prayer, fasting, suffering, Bible reading, study, meditation, worship, service, generosity, sacrifice, spiritual warfare, community, gathering, and evangelism are basic disciplines of the believer. We won't delve into all of these here, but we'll introduce a few to show how they are part of our discipleship in the faith. Donald Whitney's resource I just mentioned is my go-to for helping shape and understand the disciplines. Also, my book *Unleashed: Being Conformed to the Image of Christ* outlines how prayer grows intimacy with God and helps break out His will.[15]

Bible reading, study, and meditation give comprehensive training on the Christian life. They grow our intimacy with God and ground us in truth. That is why 2 Timothy 3:16–17 says, "All Scripture is inspired by God and is profitable for teaching, for rebuking, for correcting, for training in righteousness, so that the man of God may be complete, equipped for every good work." There are endless benefits to the fruit those disciplines serve in our lives. Spiritual disciplines exist to grow not just us but others as well. They edify the church, help promote the gospel, and model Christlikeness in its deepest form. Gathering as a community of faith reminds us that we were restored not only to God but also to one another. God didn't save us to be with Him by ourselves. That is why Paul talks about the breaking of the dividing wall to make one new humanity in Jesus (see Ephesians 2:14).

MEANS OF DISCIPLESHIP

Jesus's approach to discipleship wasn't one-dimensional. He used multifaceted means to invest in His followers. He employed all the parts of learning for His disciples: tactile (passing out fish), auditory/didactic (listening to teaching), and visual (miracles). He even employed those means simultaneously. In John 11, when Jesus got to the tomb of Lazarus, while teaching His disciples that He is the Resurrection and the life, He prayed to the Father and then told Lazarus to come forth. Mary and Martha, dear friends of Jesus and sisters of Lazarus, both heard what He said and also saw Him work, giving them an object lesson through both audi- tory and visual learning. He did the same with feeding the five thousand, healing the paralytic and the blind men, causing the storm to cease, and casting out demons. From lessons on faith to lessons of God being a provider, Jesus prepared His disciples by not only telling them about God but also showing them what it looks like to follow Him. Our disciple making must be more comprehensive than it is right now. Bible study, Sunday sermons, and small groups are wonderful and central means of disciple- ship; however, we have to be more intentional with the other means we have available to us to help truth stick and become part of our DNA.

It is not enough to teach people evangelism; we have to get them out in the street and show them how it's done. Our lessons must encompass visual aids that illustrate and drive home truths. Discipleship is the following:

- Christological—Jesus, our example (Romans 8:29)
- Relational—organic connection (John 1:35–51)
- Prototypical—modeling (Philippians 4:8–9)
- Educational—doctrinal (Colossians 1:28)
- Scriptural—sola scriptura (1 Corinthians 4:6)
- Communal—proximal and "one another-ing" (Acts 2:42–47)
- Spiritual—driven by the Holy Spirit (Ephesians 5:18–20)
- Sacrificial—commitment (Romans 12:1–2)
- Cultural—contextual (1 Corinthians 9)
- Universal—holistic (1 Thessalonians 5:23)

I hope you see that discipleship is multifaceted and multidi- mensional. First, discipleship is **Christological,** which means Jesus is our example (in Latin, *Christus Exemplar*). Paul says in

Romans 8:29 that God has "predestined [us] to be conformed to the image of his Son." Jesus sets the tone for image bearing.

Discipleship is also **relational,** meaning it requires organic connection with others. It involves taking initiative for your own spiritual formation. You're not waiting for somebody to call you and pick you up; you put yourself in situations where you have relational contact with other people. That means you make yourself available. You have to build your life around saying, *I'm going to connect with other people who happen to be believers and who are from the same local community, because we're on a mission together and God has called us in covenant together, so let's do this together.*

The idea is to be around other peers and experienced believers to support one another and share life together as you each follow Jesus. That helped me grow exponentially as a young Christian. I had a management job on campus while in college and took twenty-one credits in the fall of my senior year and nineteen in the spring in order to graduate on time. While doing that, I was active in the local church as a member. I was in the young adult choir, was a youth volunteer, and went to classes at the church. That helped me build great relationships in the church. Those relationships were the foundation of my growth. I'm not saying you need to be at church every day, but I'm saying place yourself in spheres where you can know and be known.

Discipleship is also **prototypical,** meaning it requires modeling. Paul says, "The things you have learned and received and heard and seen in me, practice these things, and the God of peace will be with you" (Philippians 4:9, NASB). As stated earlier, Jesus many times communicates His expectations through both lips and life: "This is my command: Love one another as I have loved you" (John 15:12). Peter also says, "You were called to this, because Christ also suffered for you, leaving you an example, that you should follow in his steps" (1 Peter 2:21). Modeling builds culture. Paul makes that clear to the Corinthians, who allowed a licentious culture to reign in the church: "Your boasting is not good. Don't you know that a little leaven leavens the whole batch of dough? Clean out the old leaven so that you may be a new unleavened batch, as indeed you are. For Christ our Passover lamb has been sacrificed" (1 Corinthians 5:6–7). What we encourage, challenge, reinforce, and ignore is what builds culture. You can teach sound doctrine all you want, but if you aren't living a sound life, it won't matter. Culture building must be intentional, and modeling coupled with sound teaching is paramount.

Next, discipleship is **educational.** It's doctrinal and it's **scriptural.** The Bible says, "We proclaim him, warning and teaching everyone with all wisdom, so that we may present everyone mature in Christ" (Colossians 1:28). Thus, Paul warned the church at Corinth "not to go beyond what is written" (1 Corinthians 4:6, ESV). Our church has created an environment where we ask people what they think about Scripture. Many times in Sunday school and in small groups, leaders ask what members think an interpretation of Scripture is and give almost equal weight to everyone's take even though there is only one true interpretation of Scripture. Nothing wrong with asking questions, but truth has to be clarified to limit confusion. Application is another animal: There are often many ways a passage of Scripture can be accurately applied to our lives. We must strive to understand what the authors of Scripture intended to communicate to their original audience. Before we can know how to live out the Bible, we have to have an accurate understanding of what the text says. Many believers base their views of truth on feelings or the so-called anointing of a person. We must have the discernment to see past what we *feel* the Bible says and instead hold fast to what is biblically accurate for our lives and souls.

In other words, we must demand that leaders explain what

the text is saying, not what we think or feel it is saying. Leaders shouldn't be asking, "How do you feel about loving your neighbor?" We don't ask how you *feel* about being a disciple. We don't ask how you feel about giving yourself as a living sacrifice. We don't ask how you feel as you suffer as a good Christian. Don't base your understanding of the Bible on your feelings. I don't *feel* like making peace with people who have hurt or harmed me, but what does the Bible say?

One of the things I find encouraging about the members of my church is that they will often ask me for resources for further study. They understand that I don't have time to answer every question or go in-depth on every topic, so they request a more extensive study or ask how they can dig deeper themselves. Suggest that your leaders provide teachings that nurture your heart, mind, and soul. It blesses me as a shepherd when God's people do that. It is one small way you can bless the pastors and other spiritual leaders in your life.

In light of this, we have to make sure the Word of God in its true context is communicated. Scripture always sets the tone for discipleship. In discipleship, all of us, like the Bereans in Acts, need to develop into educated listeners (see Acts 17:11). I take pride in those in my church who are genuinely passionate about walking with Jesus and seek clarity or give respectful pushback. I've made public corrections because of solid believers' being royal priests as men and women of God by lovingly speaking up about something I'd said that was off.

Disciple making is also **communal.** Proximity matters. It isn't enough for us to meet on Zoom. Virtual community doesn't allow for comprehensive spiritual growth. I'm not just talking about attending church programs; I'm saying we should find ways to engage in both organized and organic times of gathering with other believers—everything from going out together, helping one another move, celebrating birthdays, taking sanctified trips, and doing things that build memories. One means of being communal that I've found to be helpful in bringing people close quickly is retreats: Weekends where people get away from everything and are able to unplug from the hustle and bustle of life provide an injection of gospel community. The men's and women's retreats at our church have provided many a much-needed deep communal connection to Jesus and His followers. I've seen many wayward people's lives change after a communal encounter with God on these occasions.

Disciple making is **spiritual.** It must be driven by the Holy Spirit. We can't fix one another; rather, we must care for one another in a Spirit-driven atmosphere. Ephesians 5:18–20 uses one of the "one another" commands to show that discipleship is a means of others being filled with the Spirit. When I say Spirit-filled, I mean being under the control of the Spirit.

Effective discipleship is also **sacrificial.** It has to be sacrificial. That means it's not always going to be comfortable. We must rebrand discipleship so that being sacrificial is the foremost attribute. Dietrich Bonhoeffer said it best:

> The cross is not the terrible end to an otherwise godfearing and happy life, but it meets us at the beginning of our communion with Christ. When Christ calls a man, he bids him come and die. It may be a death like that of the first disciples who had to leave home and work to follow him, or it may be a death like Luther's, who had to leave the monastery and go out into the world. But it is the same death every time—death in Jesus Christ, the death of the old man at his call.[16]

Today, the only time many of the popular preachers talk about sacrifice is when it is a lure for personal success or exaltation. We have to recognize that sacrifice was actually one of the most central themes when Jesus taught on discipleship. He says, "If anyone comes to me and does not hate his own father and mother, wife and children, brothers and sisters—yes, and even his own life—he cannot be my disciple" (Luke 14:26). His point is that our love for Him should be so intense that, by comparison, our love for others resembles hate. The Lord also says, "Whoever does not bear his own cross and come after me cannot be my disciple" (verse 27). There are myriad statements that Jesus makes during His earthly ministry that scream sacrifice. We must escape the "me-centered" philosophies that plague the reels and shorts online. I'm glad some among the younger generation are starting to notice these selfish philosophies, point them out, and demand more depth and substance that calls them to growth through sacrificial living. That is happening because they are tired of commercial Christianity. Many of them tell me to keep the real Christian faith coming, not the fluff that goes viral.

Discipleship is also **cultural.** Why is it cultural? Because it looks different in different contexts but should have the same goal. It's not going to look the same in the suburbs or rural areas as it does in urban areas or even an inner-city area with a city center or downtown. For instance, when we first started our church, I was asked by a church planter friend what we would be doing for community. Would we do small groups? I told him that I didn't know, because in an inner-city area, people opening their homes to strangers might not be something they are comfortable with, particularly when attendees might act like they are going to the bathroom but are actually robbing their hosts. My friend was blown away. The important principle is to prioritize community, not a certain model. We must make sure we customize ministry to the particular context we are called to without losing the gospel and the truth of the Word. As Paul states,

Although I am free from all and not anyone's slave, I have made myself a slave to everyone, in order to win more people. To the Jews I became like a Jew, to win Jews; to those under the law, like one under the law—though I myself am not under the law—to win those under the law. To those who are without the law, like one without the law—though I am not without God's law but under the law of Christ—to win those without the law. To the weak I became weak, in order to win the weak. I have become all things to all people, so that I may by every possible means save some. (1 Corinthians 9:19–22)

Paul doesn't adjust the gospel; he adjusts the means, or the tools of communication, action, and execution.

And finally, discipleship is **universal.** When I say discipleship is universal, I mean it's holistic. Our whole person must be changed by the gospel: "May the God of peace himself sanctify you completely. And may your whole spirit, soul, and body be kept sound and blameless at the coming of our Lord Jesus Christ" (1 Thessalonians 5:23). The point is, God wants us comprehensively changed in every area of life.

As a believer in Jesus Christ, you have a right and duty to desire that discipleship bleed into everything the church does. Discipleship is the central task Jesus has given the church (see Matthew 28:18–20), so I would say that a church or ministry that doesn't have a clear disciple-making philosophy isn't worthy of your time and investment. If you are attending a church that doesn't have a clear vision for discipleship, it is likely time to consider another place of worship. A fog in the pulpit will be blindness in the pew. Use this chapter as a rubric of sorts to aid you in making a healthy judgment when it comes to discipleship and finding a local church.

However, maybe you attend a church with a heart for discipleship, but you've been content to remain on the outside looking in. I want to challenge you to take a step of faith this week. Consider one way you could connect more deeply in community at your church, or perhaps you could discuss spiritual disciplines with someone whose faith you admire. Ask for advice about incorporating one of the spiritual disciplines into your daily routine. Discipleship is the most important task Jesus has given us, and it is not a spectator sport.

5

REBRANDING PREACHING AND TEACHING

AS MY WIFE AND I HAVE RAISED OUR FOUR CHILDREN, I HAVE WON-
dered how they are processing their upbringing and how they
will respond in the future to the way they were raised. I have a
son in his early twenties who is now in college. When raising
kids, some of your greatest angst comes when they leave the
house. It's a blessing and a challenge at the same time.

It's a blessing because they are out. Time to go. Amen! Time to
transition! But it's a challenge because you are always curious
about how they're doing. You are also hoping you prepared them
well enough to become independent. You wonder, *Did I sufficiently
equip them? Was there a lesson I failed to teach them? Did I do enough to invest
in their future?* That's why John says, "I have no greater joy than this:
to hear that my children are walking in truth" (3 John 1:4). He
is speaking about his *spiritual* children, but it applies to the actual
children in our care as well.

In 2 Corinthians 11, Paul shares some of his greatest trials:
shipwrecks, sleepless nights, being pelted with rocks and left for

dead, and being run out of town by the very people he came to serve. However, he says he is most burdened about the health of local churches. One of my heaviest burdens as a pastor is concern for how the church body is doing.

Along those lines, some questions I have for you are about discernment: Do you have a clear sense of your own spiritual health? Are you ingesting truth, or are you just going to church? In other words, is Christ being formed in you? Are you growing? Is there visible movement closer to Jesus? Are your attitudes, perspectives, and passions being shaped by Him? Are you progressively living more like Him, or do you just go to church to settle your conscience and then roll out?

Perhaps more than any other letter Paul wrote, 2 Corinthians expresses his frustration. He was upset because the church at Corinth was gullible. Their lack of discernment kept Paul up at night. This church's lack of maturity grieved Paul. He said, "I am jealous for you with a godly jealousy, because I have promised you in marriage to one husband—to present a pure virgin to Christ" (11:2).

Paul had invested deeply in this church, spending about a year and a half in Corinth leading them to Jesus and teaching them what it looks like to follow Him. He not only taught them but also showed them what it meant to be healthy, maturing, and discerning believers.

Notice that "Paul spoke of having a 'godly jealousy' for them (verse 2). What does that mean? It means he was not jealous in a petty sense but rather was expressing intense, fatherly concern that the Corinthians stay true to their relationship with God."[1]

It is worth noting that "Being jealous over God's people with God's jealousy would have been viewed as pious. Fathers normally pledged their daughters in marriage, and Paul compares the Corinthian church with a daughter whom he has pledged in marriage to Christ; later Jewish depictions of God marrying his son Israel to the law."[2] Paul was venting his rage over intruding false teachers who came into Corinth and led people astray after he had put in so much work to ensure they had an abundant walk with the Lord.

As a pastor and leader in the body of Christ and someone who invests in other pastors, I feel this same rage at times. I feel it because I have prayerfully labored in God's presence to carefully craft messages, content, and resources to lead people to spiritual health, only to see them so easily led astray. I've seen people in church make significant strides in following Jesus, only to later see them post, affirm, and promote false teaching. Our church has invested deeply in people who have deconstructed their faith under the influence of false teaching videos they found on YouTube.

We live in a world of rampant biblical illiteracy. Disciples of Jesus must be discerning more than ever because the Enemy is very active. One speaker was recently asked what the greatest threat to the church is. He said, "Pastors."[3] He even talks about how there are many church leaders who are biblically illiterate, morally bankrupt, or unconverted. I agree wholeheartedly. I'd add that those types are perfect conduits for Satan's devices.

Paul says, "I fear that, as the serpent deceived Eve by his cunning, your minds may be seduced from a sincere and pure devotion to Christ" (2 Corinthians 11:3). Sadly, I see that all the time in our age of internet experts. The apostle is concerned about people in the church being sold a different Jesus: "If a person comes and preaches another Jesus, whom we did not preach, or you receive a different spirit, which you had not received, or a different gospel, which you had not accepted, you put up with it splendidly!" (verse 4). One of the greatest challenges is that our Lord is presented by many teachers as existing for us rather than us existing for Him.

WHAT IS EXPOSITIONAL PREACHING?

As a new believer in college, I really loved the preaching portion in church. I had a hunger like no other to understand the Bible. I'd spend hours daily in the Word, devouring it. When it was time for the sermon, I had my Bible and notepad ready. Everyone seemed to have a different style and approach to preaching and teaching the text. Because I was young in the faith, I didn't know any formal categories; all I wanted was to know the Word, apply it to my life, and share it with others. As time went on, if a preacher got up and read Scripture but didn't explain it, I'd blank out and start studying and reading the text on my own during the sermon. One time a preacher came to our church and walked through a passage in Philippians 3. I was astounded at how simply and clearly he walked through the text. He was explaining the Bible in context and helping us apply it to our lives. From that day on, I knew that was the type of preaching I wanted to hear. I soon discovered there was a name for it: *expositional preaching.*

I had the honor of sitting under the expositional preaching of Dr. Tony Evans for about a decade. I learned about exposition in school, but there was nothing like being in the restaurant watching the chef cook and then give you a meal. I like to read cookbooks, but I like to eat what's in the book as well. While I was a student at Dallas Theological Seminary, we went through every book of the Bible expositionally. It was an honor and treat that made my journey as a disciple even more amazing. What then is expositional preaching? According to American theologian Haddon Robinson,

> Expository preaching is the communication of a biblical concept, derived from and transmitted through a historical, grammatical, and literary study of a passage in its context, which the

Holy Spirit first applies to the personality and experience of the preacher, then through the preacher, applies to the hearers.[4]

David Helm is a pastor and the founder of Charles Simeon Trust, an organization dedicated to training people to preach and study the Bible expositionally. Helm says, "Expositional preaching is empowered preaching that rightfully submits the shape and emphasis of the sermon to the shape and emphasis of a biblical text. . . . It brings out of the text what the Holy Spirit put there . . . and does not put into the text what the preacher *thinks* might be there" (emphasis added).[5] In other words, *the Bible* drives the focus of the preaching, not the preacher.

This is where I get concerned with much of the topical preaching today: Many pastors do only topical messages that lend themselves more readily to eisegesis. "This can often mean coming to the Scripture with a biased cultural lens that didn't exist during the time the Bible was written. Of course, theologians frown upon this approach because it isn't rooted in Scripture."[6] Also, it can involve finding scriptures that say what you want to say and presenting them out of context. It can also simply be misunderstanding Scripture altogether. I find people benefit more from preaching that explains the text, points people to Jesus and the gospel, and helps with life application.

A BALANCED DIET

My father in the ministry taught us to give the congregation a vast biblical diet. He encouraged us to preach through books of the Bible, doctrines of the faith/systematic theology, topical expositions on felt needs, and topical expositions on current events that may need addressing. I can truly say that as I sat under the teachings of Dr. Evans, I received a balanced diet. You need to be able to discern truth, and you can do that only if you learn the Bible well. And if you are a leader in the church, you should be training God's people on what to expect and how to listen.

All followers of Jesus must learn how to hear. We must develop the ability to understand the difference between truth and falsehood. We are royal priests of the living God (see 1 Peter 2:9) and have an anointing from Him. John speaks of the Holy Spirit giving the people of God discernment to understand His Word and discern truth well (see 1 John 4:1–6). In Acts 17:11, the Bereans were called noble because they checked even what the apostle Paul taught. If you hear something in church that seems off, don't be afraid to search the Bible to make sure what you are hearing is true. No preacher or teacher is above examination of what they communicate. And to be honest, if the leaders of your church get offended by you checking their teaching against the Bible, that is a huge red flag.

I pray that you and I can usher in an era when believers have a hunger for truth that pulsates, calling the pulpit up. I pray there will be a demand for substance above fluff. I believe I see that time coming. On the other hand, I pray we don't become stale and stoic in orthodoxy, with no passion and no love of Christ and His mission. On that note, I think felt-need messages do have a place in the church at times.

Faithful felt-need messages tend to flow from being with the sheep and exegeting culture. Healthy felt-needs sermons involve hearing what people are dealing with in their daily lives and seeking God in His Word for wisdom to address those issues biblically. Such messages help people understand the heart and mind of God regarding issues they face. Unhealthy felt-need sermons conform the message to appease people's personal preferences and desires regardless of biblical principles. When it comes to important issues people are facing in my church, I want to help God's people know that the Bible deals with real life. Topical series should help believers see how biblical principles give us wisdom to navigate matters the Bible might not explicitly address. For instance, when medical marijuana was legalized in our state, I wanted to help my church navigate that biblically. And even though the Bible doesn't directly address marijuana use, there are principles in Scripture that can help us think with a Christian mindset about the issue. As drinking became more normalized, I felt it was important to address that from the pulpit. Even many Christians today don't view foul language as cursing because cursing in the Bible is different. In light of those developments, I decided to do a series on Christian liberties.

Disciple making must deal with where people are. Jesus preached topically in the Gospels. Paul preached topically. The writers of the New Testament wrote topically, using the Old Testament texts. In the Sermon on the Mount (see Matthew 5–7), Jesus was preaching topically on the subject of "You have heard it said." In doing so, He dealt with an array of subjects from personal relationships to giving and prayer. Then He applied the principles to other areas in the lives of the recipients. All sermons, whether topical or exegetical, should be textual. Preaching topically doesn't give someone permission to take Scripture out of context. It should always let the truth of God's Word, and not anyone's personal agenda, take center stage.

Current events can be touchy subjects, particularly in our cultural context. However, Jesus didn't shy away from current events of His time, nor did the prophets and apostles. In Luke 13:4, Jesus addresses the incident of the tower of Siloam, where the tower collapsed and killed eighteen people. There was speculation that it was God's judgment on them. Whether it is a political delegation in Isaiah coming from Babylon or Daniel engaging the governing leaders in Persia and Babylon, there are going to be things that happen around us that need theological engagement.

Even those walking on the road to Emmaus were talking with Jesus about the Crucifixion as a current event—something everyone was talking about and trying to get clarity on. That doesn't mean that every current cultural event should be mentioned on Sunday, but events that relate to or influence our Christian worldview may need to be addressed, particularly if they are causing anxiety or division in the church.

Whether it's about police brutality, racism, injustice, equal rights, abortion policies, birth control, or immigration, Christians must not be cowards when speaking truth to power. Isaiah addressed widespread social issues in Israel and engaged them biblically:

> Woe to those enacting crooked statutes
> and writing oppressive laws
> to keep the poor from getting a fair trial
> and to deprive the needy among my people of justice,
> so that widows can be their spoil
> and they can plunder the fatherless.
> (Isaiah 10:1–2)

When I've done series that give the Bible's viewpoint on particular cultural matters, many people say, "I didn't realize how many things Scripture addresses." When we thoughtfully speak about current events in light of the gospel, it communicates to believers and unbelievers alike that Scripture is relevant and powerful in every area and age of life.

RESTORING SOLID HERMENEUTICS TO THE PULPIT

Public worship and gatherings play vital roles in the church's culture building and stability. People often base their primary decision to join a church largely on the Sunday morning experience: the music, the preaching and teaching, and the children's ministry offerings. The preaching of the Word is one of the most important mechanisms for the church. In 2 Timothy 4:1–2, Paul says, "I solemnly charge you before God and Christ Jesus, who is going to judge the living and the dead, and because of his appearing and his kingdom: Preach the word; be ready in season and out of season; correct, rebuke, and encourage with great patience and teaching." Those are Paul's last words, and he could have said a billion things, but he chose "Preach the word!" He even shared with Timothy how important the Word is and what its uses are (see 2 Timothy 3:14–17). Paul was about to be executed for his faith, and he wanted to leave his spiritual son with what's most important.

Remember the well-known pastor I mentioned in chapter 3 who stated in a reel on Instagram and on YouTube that theology and exegesis aren't important? He made it seem as though those things aren't spiritual and reduce God to intellectual interpretation. It was bad! The Bible speaks on study in verses like Ezra 7:10 and 2 Timothy 2:15. Even Peter makes it clear that maximizing preaching the Word is a core role of leaders and they must not be pulled away from it (see Acts 6:2). Paul talks about asking the Colossians to pray for His ability to be clear in gospel preaching (see Colossians 4:3–4). You, as a parishioner, owe it to your soul to be in a context where your leaders are prepared. If they are not, it's not a church you should continue to attend. If prophecy and the sign gifts are given more emphasis than the preaching of God's Word, you need to find another place where you can grow spiritually.

Paul commands Timothy to "preach . . . in season and out of season" (2 Timothy 4:2)—when people want to listen and when they don't; when it's popular and when it's not.

We should also talk about what Paul calls "rightly dividing the word of truth" (2 Timothy 2:15, NKJV), which refers to accurately understanding and interpreting the Bible. There are many people out there "rightly dividing the word of truth." However, what's popular and what goes viral tend to be the things that are less sound. Hermeneutics is the art and science of interpreting Scripture, and rightly interpreting the Bible is vital to spiritual health. Unfortunately, we live in an age of self-centered hermeneutics. Paul said that this day would come. The focus of many churches right now is man, not Jesus. You can listen to whole messages and not hear about Jesus, the gospel, or accurate principles from the Word. That is why it is written, "The time will come when people will not tolerate sound doctrine, but according to their own desires, will multiply teachers for themselves because they have an itch to hear what they want to hear. They will turn away from hearing the truth and will turn aside to myths" (4:3–4).

Paul gives Timothy a most solemn charge to carry out: to faithfully and consistently preach the full Word based on the certain return of Christ and His kingdom, and the certain knowledge of opposition even within the church (see verses 2–5). Once again, we see that the early church was threatened by serious apostasy and divisive teaching, which Paul says will satisfy only the cravings of those who reject "sound doctrine" in place of "myths."[7] Craig Keener notes that the "term translated *myths* was usually used derogatorily for false stories."[8]

Paul outlines two results of spiritual wandering. First, the listeners would turn away from hearing the truth of the gospel (see 2:18). Second, they would "turn aside to myths" (4:4). The verb translated *turn aside* is a medical term used to describe wrenching a limb out of joint.[9] The term *myths* is a reference to all those religious errors that can flood the minds of the listeners because they desire to turn away from the truth. "Because they looked for someone to soothe the itch rather than to satisfy the thirst, they would leave the truth without an awareness of their desertion."[10]

These myths come from bad hermeneutics and exegesis: "Exegesis consists of the actual interpretation of the Bible, the bringing out of its meaning, whereas hermeneutics establishes the principles by which exegesis is practiced."[11] "First, hermeneutics is a science, since it provides a logical, orderly classification of the laws of interpretation. . . . Second, hermeneutics is an art, for it is an acquired skill demanding both imagination and an ability to apply the 'laws' to selected passages or books."[12] At the end of the day, we need preachers and teachers who are biblically responsible.

There are many people out there who are really irresponsible with the Bible, and sadly they get a ton of press. I recently watched a video compilation of false teachers.[13] In the video one preacher says Adam was made more perfect than Jesus.[14] Another says we were brought into the Godhead—that we became gods.[15] There is some rampant teaching going around that suggests under the Old Covenant, we served God, but in the New Covenant, God serves us. Yet another person says that our hearts are the Holy of Holies. Each one of those theories comes from a lack of understanding of the nature of biblical interpretation and how the Bible reveals truth. God serves us in both the Old Testament and the New Testament. The Old Testament testifies that God created the Sabbath for us. It talks about God's promises to shepherd and provide for us and much more. Similarly, in the New Testament, Jesus says that He came to serve. In both testaments, we are called to serve the Lord. We serve Him with gladness. In the New Testament, Jesus says, "The greatest among you will be your servant" (Matthew 23:11). If we are going to consume online content, it should be sound doctrine and even those who warn us about false teachers. Some sources for these warnings are Jackie and Preston Perry,

Allen Parr, Jerome Gay, KB and Ameen of Southside Rabbi, Damon Richardson, and other great apologetics channels. BibleProject is amazing for all ages as a visual tool to understand the Bible in context.

Do what you need to do to grow your kingdom IQ. Take a Bible-study-methods class online or ask your pastors and leaders to sponsor a session of them teaching it at your church. One of the most important things you must understand is that you need to learn not just *what* to think but also *how* to think. You don't need a seminary degree or familiarity with Greek and Hebrew to learn how to interpret the Bible, but you do need to take time to consider the context of any passage of Scripture you are studying. Ask yourself, *Who was the original audience of this book of the Bible, and what was this author trying to communicate to them?* And if you don't know the answer to those questions, ask a church leader. Or maybe even ask a church leader for a recommendation of a good Bible commentary. Read Scripture prayerfully and thoughtfully. Try to understand the intended meaning of the text before you start applying it to your life. On the flip side, don't stop at simply understanding the Bible's meaning; according to James, even the demons understand important truths about God (see James 2:19). Once you have a handle on what the passage means, take time to journal or pray about how God might be moving you to apply it to your everyday life. Also, Logos, a Bible-study platform and app, has many levels that regular believers are able to use to learn how to study the Bible accurately and effectively. The company even hosts seminars on how to use their platform.

METHODS OF INTERPRETING SCRIPTURE

Great and helpful preaching and teaching starts with solid biblical interpretation. Study the Bible to uncover what the author intended to communicate rather than just what you think it means. When we understand that, we have uncovered something powerful and profound: We have uncovered what the God of the universe wants to teach us. It is an approach that has been used for millennia by biblical interpreters for the church. It shouldn't be complicated; it should be accessible and understandable. "The literal sense is the grammatical-historical sense, that is, the meaning which the writer expressed."[16] *Literal* also covers every genre, and "it doesn't mean that everything in the Bible is meant to be taken literally. It more so means exactness of meaning in interpretation."[17] "Interpretation according to the literal sense will take account of all figures of speech and literary forms found in the text."[18]

After observing a text, it is important to use Bible dictionaries, concordances, background commentaries, lexicons, and study Bibles to get to the meaning of the text. These tools will help transport you back to authorial intent and help you understand how the original audience would have understood the text. Once you understand the author's original intent and context, you can then move to the important work of applying the text to life today. This section and what follows will help point us to proper methods of interpretation.

Grammatical

When studying the Bible, we must pay attention to grammar and style. We also need to understand the genre of the book of the Bible we are reading. That is particularly important when studying books that are poetic, prophetic, or apocalyptic. These genres employ symbols and figures of speech and must be interpreted accordingly. When we fail to properly take genre into consideration, we can make massive errors. For instance, Black Hebrew Israelites use Revelation 1:14–17 to say that Jesus is black. They use the phrase "His feet were like fine bronze as it is fired in a furnace" (verse 15) to justify their position, but that phrase is "a figure of speech intended to communicate something about His character and nature. Most likely the phrase denotes moral purity."[19] That doesn't necessarily mean Jesus wasn't a man of color, but it's a lesson in how personal bias can affect Bible interpretation.

Historical

Historical means that the books of the Bible were written at particular junctures in history, and the historical cultural background of the Bible's authors must be considered in our interpretation. When I was in college, I used to get roasted by non-Christians about the nails being put in Jesus's hands. They said the nails would tear through His hands and would not support His weight. However, I told them that in Jewish culture, hands were considered to extend from the fingertips to the elbows. And when you study Roman crucifixion, nails were driven through the wrists, not what we call hands.[20]

Redemptive-Historical

Redemptive-historical points to how the Bible's narrative shows God's saving work in multifaceted ways. The Bible is not two different plans for two different peoples of God (i.e., Jews and Christians). All Scripture, whether in the Old or New Testament, not only points to but also reveals Jesus as the center of the narrative and helps readers apply the implications of Jesus's ultimate lordship. Jesus says, "You pore over the Scriptures because you think you have eternal life in them, and yet they testify about me" (John 5:39). Acts tells us that Jesus, on the road to Emmaus, reveals how all Scripture centers on Him: "Beginning with Moses and all the

Prophets, he interpreted for them the things concerning himself in all the Scriptures" (Luke 24:27). Biblical scholar Sidney Greidanus notes that "the Old Testament proclaims God's mighty acts of redemption. These acts reach a climax in the New Testament when God sends his Son. Redemptive history is the mighty river that runs from the old covenant to the new and holds the two together."[21]

Preaching needs to be Christ-centered and gospel-centered. The church today is in need of a revival of sound preaching and teaching. I'm sick of the nonsense that so often passes for "truth" in many churches. I believe that we have been given spiritual gifts, but they can never outshine the Word of God. That is why Paul says, "These things, brethren, I have figuratively applied to myself and Apollos for your sakes, so that in us you may learn not to exceed what is written, so that no one of you will become arrogant in behalf of one against the other" (1 Corinthians 4:6, NASB). Prophecy, words of wisdom and knowledge, and interpretation of tongues must be submitted to the clear teaching of the Bible, and any message that contradicts it should be rejected.

Centrally, rebranding preaching and teaching is, in many ways, in the hands of the people of God just as much as it is in the hands of the church leaders. Don't give audience to false teaching, preaching, and prophecy. When I was growing up, there was a grocery store in my neighborhood that sold terrible and expired products. You could smell how spoiled they were when you walked in. Although it was the closest grocery store to us, we ended up going out of our neighborhood for better options. When we found a store that cared more about the food it sold, we ended up committing to shopping there. Many people followed suit. Not too long after that, the first store closed. In a similar way, place yourself in a healthy, biblically sound environment. Refusing to give audience to an unhealthy place will bankrupt it.

It's possible that you will need to find a new church home. For example, if your church is regularly promoting false teaching, you should leave immediately and find a church that teaches the Bible faithfully and accurately. I am not, however, saying that you should leave your church if your pastor merely says something you disagree with. Remember that pastors are fallible and are going to say things from the pulpit that you disagree with or even think are wrong. There is a difference between the occasional point of disagreement and a sustained pattern of mishandling the Word of God. It is okay to disagree with your pastor on secondary and tertiary issues. However, if you and your pastor can't agree on who Jesus is and why He came to earth, that's a big problem and an indication that you need to make a change. There is a difference between sustained false teaching and the occasional preaching blunder. I love how the members of my church encourage me and hold me accountable to faithfully teaching the Bible. Remember that all the "one another" commands in the Bible also apply to how you interact with your pastor. Strive to love, encourage, and support your pastor in the teaching and preaching ministry of your church.

When people tell me they are moving away and will no longer be able to attend our church, I always ask them why they are moving. They'll often say that it's for a job opportunity, and I'll show excitement for them. However, once they've moved away and been gone for a while, I will check on them and ask, "Did you find a solid church community that you could connect with?" Many times, the answer is no. I often encourage people to think not just of their financial life in a move but also their soul. Soul health is connected to a biblically healthy environment that flows from healthy preaching and teaching. Healthy rebranding requires that we demand a healthy pulpit. Some of those spaces might not be large and popular, and others might be. I pray that every believer will find a healthy environment in which to grow and put their hand to the plow for the kingdom of God.

6

REBRANDING PURPOSE AND DREAMING

WHO AM I? WHAT'S MY PURPOSE? WHAT'S MY VALUE? EVERYONE WRES-tles with these three questions. Each represents an important sector of our lives: identity, significance, and dignity.

Identity: Who am I?

Significance: What's my purpose?

Dignity: What's my value?

I know I have ragged on the tactics of many modern preachers, but I will admit that these preachers often have their fingers on the pulse of culture. For example, if I wanted to make sure my next sermons amass more than a hundred thousand views, and if I want to pack the church with tons of new visitors, there are three topics that are going to be fire and capture people's attention: money, relationships, and purpose.

Discussions of purpose and dreaming are embedded into so many sermons these days. It seems to me that we have made purpose our purpose. A lot of preachers have begun worshipping their own personal value and encouraging their people to do the same. If we're not careful, we will begin worshipping our own significance and pursuing our own self-designated purpose. In other words, when we worship our own significance and elevate our own purpose, we lose sight of God—the identity He has given us, the significance of His purpose for us, and the dignity of bearing His image and being redeemed by Him.

Why is that type of preaching so detrimental to the church and its witness? It's all about "me"—it is self-centered! We live in a culture that loves to elevate personal desires. In 2 Timothy 3, Paul warns about how so many people are becoming lovers of self. Then in chapter 4, he admonishes against the temptation all people face to find teachers who preach what they desire to hear. What is wrong with seeking those kinds of preachers? Why did Paul warn Timothy against that? Seeking those preachers is problematic, in part, because many people perceive sermons from the perspective of what they want to gain from God. They elevate the "natural" over the spiritual to the peril of all who hear. Many of those sermons are absent of any mention of sin and make everything the fault of the haters. In addition, that preaching assumes that Satan's primary goal is to stop our personal destinies rather than to oppose the work of Christ's kingdom, which is the making of disciples and pointing people to Jesus.

In other words, I think there is a real problem today of the pulpit becoming overly focused on self and people's personal journeys rather than on God, His people, and His purposes for us. Everyone loves to think about themselves and how they might make their lives better. If we aren't careful, Sunday sermons can turn into motivational speeches rather than gospel-focused declarations of God's Word. And that type of preaching is deeply misleading because it can actually drive a lot of counterproductive church growth that we will interpret as God's favor, whereas in reality, we have merely used Jesus to give people what they want.

We must realize that simply being busy isn't our purpose. From a biblical standpoint, we should be able to develop and understand a beautiful framework for our purpose, rooted in God's Word, because Scripture has already made our purpose clear.

I've read the Bible from cover to cover many times, and sometimes stuff just jumps out at me differently. Once, I was reading Exodus devotionally and I came upon Exodus 30:22–33. It was talking about how God had the priests make incense and perfumes and essentially said, "Listen, nobody is to make these outside their designated purpose." And then He said, "It must not be applied to people's bodies, and you must not make any like it with the same recipe. It is holy, and it must be holy to you. Whoever makes perfume like it and whoever puts any of it on someone not a priest will be cut off from his people" (verses 32–33, NET). In my mind, all they did was mix some herbs and spices together. But as I began to meditate on the passage, I realized that God is a beast of a brander; He was letting us know that no one else can have the rights to that recipe. In essence, the incense and perfume were used in the tabernacle to be an aromatic expression and fragrance for God.

My question was, Why was He so serious about making sure nobody ever used the oil in an unauthorized way? Why was He concerned that these perfumes not be used for other purposes outside worship? After dwelling on that for a while, it hit me. It was as if God said to me, "I wanted the scent from the tabernacle of Israel to have a unique fragrance that no other place had." In other words, His people are supposed to smell different from everybody else. It was as if He were saying, "I can't have any unauthorized people acting like they're Mine. I want My people to be branded—to smell a certain way." God wants His disciples to be distinctly and noticeably different such that we leave a gospel-shaped impression on those we interact with.

PLAYING INTO PEOPLE'S HEDONISM AND NARCISSISM

Most people think of the church and preachers as money-hungry. And let's be honest: Many are. Before social media, sources such as Black Entertainment Television (BET), the Word Network, Trinity Broadcasting Network (TBN), Christian Broadcasting Network (CBN), and Daystar Television Network were the main means for the church to be seen on TV, and most of their programming seemed to be unsound. You'd have some decent content on these platforms, but what got the most attention were telethons, people selling prayer cloths, and ministries using manipulation to entice people to give money. Many of the programs were rooted in what is now known as the prosperity gospel, which has multiplied a thousandfold through social media.

The prosperity gospel has done a ton of damage to the church in both overt and covert ways.

> Proponents of this movement contend that this "faith" is the means by which believers appropriate the will of God, resulting in prosperity and success in life—better health and the blessing of wealth. The movement was founded by the teachings of Essek William Kenyon (1867–1948), whose teachings range from concerningly heterodox to egregiously heretical, and much of Kenyon's teaching was later popularized by Kenneth Hagin Sr.[1]

These teachings evolved into what is called the Word of Faith movement. Kenyon, during his time in college in New England, was

> exposed to and influenced by metaphysical cults such as New Thought, Christian Science, Unity School of Christianity, and Science of the Mind. . . .

Kenyon saw the metaphysical sciences as false religions, yet he agreed with certain ideas they had about deification, the power of the mind, and the power of faith to produce healing and overcome sickness and poverty. Kenyon sought to combine certain elements from the metaphysical sciences that he liked with Christianity in order to develop a new Christianity that underscored the power of faith to receive healing, wealth, and greater supernatural authority.[2]

Hagin would later adapt his teaching to that of Kenyon's after claiming he had an experience with God healing him from heart disease. He was an itinerate Assembly of God preacher, and his healing was in 1934. In 1950, he came into contact with books by Kenyon, and his ministry took a turn in an explosive direction. He moved from Texas to Tulsa and became one of the most influential charismatic figures of the twentieth century, influencing Frederick K. C. Price, Kenneth Copeland, and a host of others. He became the landmark leader of the charismatic movement.

Over the years, the movement has taken many forms. In the 1980s, it was Price whose broadcast influenced many. Later it was Copeland, Jesse Duplantis, Rod Parsley, Carlton Pearson, Creflo Dollar, Leroy Thompson, and many others. Today, many prominent charismatic preachers who are well known aren't as overt about their connection to the prosperity gospel, perhaps due to the bad press the movement has gotten over the years. As a result, prosperity teachers have shifted in how they exercise their influence. Although there are still the traditional prosperity folks who make outlandish asks of their followers with unprecedented promises of return, there is a new school of prosperity teachers who are much more subtle in their approach.

I had a church member who was a physician connected to

the Centers for Disease Control and Prevention counsel our church about health and safety during the pandemic. When we returned to meeting in person, I asked him about the current risk of the virus and where he thought things would be in the near future. He stated, "In many ways, it will be like the common cold. Whenever a virus realizes that it is killing its host, it re-adapts. The fundamental desire of a virus is to live and spread and grow. Therefore, it makes itself less deadly to accomplish its goal." The prosperity gospel and the Word of Faith movement are viruses, and they have deeply damaged the church. They have deceived countless people into believing that the gospel is really more about their own personal happiness, wealth, and fulfill-ment than about the glory of God and the good of the world. These movements have also damaged the church's reputation, as unbelievers have watched prosperity preachers defraud people and redefine faithfulness around material gain.

Now that people have become aware of the false promises of the prosperity gospel, it has morphed into a less potent and overt message. It now operates in the realm of subtlety. From what I've observed, messages using the following buzzwords—*purpose, dreaming, manifesting,* and *affirmations*—are driving a new iteration of prosperity preaching.

A dear friend of mine, Damon Richardson, breaks this move-ment into four quadrants: New Apostolic Reformation (seven mountains of influence), the prophetic movement, the Word of Faith movement, and the deliverance and spiritual-warfare move-ment. Each has major influence today. To understand our subject better, we have to briefly summarize these movements.

The New Apostolic Reformation

Have you noticed the sudden rise in people transitioning their titles from *pastors* to *apostles*? That is thanks to an influential movement many do not know about: the New Apostolic Reformation (NAR). Let's look into the definition of this movement:

> It's apostolic because its leaders claim they're restoring the lost office of apostle to the church—an office endowed with astonishing authority, miraculous powers, and divine strategies for establishing God's kingdom on earth. It's a reformation because proponents say the movement will completely change the way church is done, and its effects will be as great—or even greater than—the sixteenth-century Protestant Reformation. The biggest innovation of NAR is the belief that apostles, working together with prophets, must take over governance of the church—taking the reins from the pastors, elders, and denominational leaders—so that God's end-time plans can be fulfilled and Christ can return. Churches that do not submit to the authority of these present-day apostles and prophets will sit on the sidelines as mere spectators.[3]

In this movement "there are apostles in the church, but there are also what proponents of NAR call 'workplace apostles.' These are those who go into the so-called seven mountains. These mountains are government, media, family, business, education, church, and the arts."[4] It's believed, in this movement, that to fulfill our kingdom mandate, we must take dominion over these various spheres and institutions. Now, I don't disagree that these mechanisms are things God will use for His glory. But understand that the early church was primarily made up of marginalized people. God often builds His kingdom despite the surrounding systems and institutions. Consider, for example, the exponential growth Christianity is experiencing in places like China, where many aspects of practicing the Christian faith are not legal. God could overthrow authority, as He did with scores of previous governing systems, but that doesn't seem to be the way He operates in the New Covenant. And just because being identified as a Christian in certain sectors of life can be costly doesn't mean government, business, and education need to be overthrown.

The NAR essentially says that society should be changed from the top down and not from the bottom up. Proponents of this movement claim that believers are to be at the top of society, which is a form of prosperity and purpose preaching. In other words, they believe there are territorial spirits over the seven areas. And because the areas are the most influential in society, Christians need to get in these places and expel the spirits and claim them for the kingdom.

There are numerous problems with the NAR movement, but I want to briefly outline three. First, it emphasizes experience over Scripture. In many ways, these current apostles embody an authority that is not rooted in Scripture but rather is clearly outside the boundaries of biblical teachings. Second, they believe they can get new revelation, meaning the leaders of the movement believe that God gives them ideas that are equal to the Scriptures. Third, they use Ephesians 4 (particularly verse 11) and the so-called fivefold ministry (referring to the five roles that God has called Christians to fill) to state that apostles and prophets today are the highest authority in the church. That is very concerning because when Paul planted churches, he appointed elders, not apostles and prophets, to be the highest governing authority in local churches.

The Prophetic Movement

The prophetic movement is a charismatic movement that emphasizes unbiblical manifestation of the Spirit and counterfeit anointings. I believe the signs gifts (speaking in tongues, visions, healings) still exist today and haven't ceased, but I believe they are meant to be used with clear biblical parameters and accountability. In this prophetic movement, there has been a co-opting of new age teaching and forms of witchcraft that its proponents believe redeemable, like manifesting, declarations, positive confessions, grave soaking, and many other strange practices. This is affirmed in the book *The Physics of Heaven*, by Judy Franklin and Ellyn Davis.[5] Regarding that book, Dr. Christopher Berg, in *The New Age Trojan Horse*, states,

> Franklin's first sentence sums up the theological foundation of the book and Bethel's entire engagement with the New Age: "My journey into the mysteries of sound, light, vibrations, and quantum mechanics began with one word—'sound.'" Franklin, Davis, and the leaders of Bethel are not diving into the Scriptures to acquire their knowledge; rather, they are relying on a subjective inner voice experience. Davis goes on to explain, like others who engage in New Age syncretism, that "the Christianity of my childhood seemed to have little relevance to my everyday life." Thus, she sought out truth in the New Age Movement and claims that "a lot of what I saw and heard in the New Age Movement embodied biblical principles and could be backed up by Scripture." Given these statements and the endorsements and contributions to the book by key Bethel leaders, it is impossible to deny that Bethel Redding has fully embraced New Age Movement practices and attempted to syncretize them with a Christian veneer.[6]

One question might be, why does this matter? It matters because we don't have to use Satan's tools to acquire God's blessings. Author Andrew Strom, who left the prophetic movement for that reason, says,

> I have no problem with gifts of the Holy Spirit such as miracles, healing, prophecy, etc. These are found all through the Bible,

after all. But I have a big problem when "manifestations" come in that seem completely unbiblical and more like eastern New Age or "Kundalini." I am apt to get very upset when I see the Body of Christ—for whom Jesus died—getting invaded by what seem to be counterfeits or false anointings. And so, I was not a tremendously "popular" guy.[7]

Strom asserts that the movement had become deeply committed to money and false prophecies. American missionary and writer C. Peter Wagner, who was instrumental in the NAR movement, was also a proponent of the prophetic movement. He lists many of the key reasons that he was concerned:

- The giving and receiving of "ear-tickling" words.
- The giving and receiving of money in expectation of prophecy.
- False words and false teaching.
- The lack of a true Repentance message.
- The spiritual "blindness" that allows familiar spirits and spirits of divination to flourish.
- The failure of this movement to judge itself, meaning that God must judge it.
- The idolising of well-known prophets—placing them on a pedestal.[8]

I've heard people initiating prophecies on demand as if they can do so. But a more biblical phrase would be, "The word of the LORD *came* to me."[9] God the Spirit, not us, is the initiator of prophecy.

The Word of Faith Movement

Another movement that distorts the gospel and has done damage to the church's reputation today is the Word of Faith movement:

The core claims of the Word of Faith/Prosperity movement are that God's desire is for all Christians to be happy, healthy, and wealthy. These teachers often claim that God allows a person to "speak" their desires into reality, as though they had a creative power similar to that of God. Sickness, poverty, and other struggles are seen as evidence of a lack of faith.[10]

One of the foundational verses for the Word of Faith movement is "Death and life are in the power of the tongue, and those who love it will eat its fruit" (Proverbs 18:21). Another verse used and popularized is "I have made you the father of many nations—in the presence of the God in whom he believed, the one who gives life to the dead and *calls things into existence that do not exist*" (Romans 4:17). These verses are used to promote the false doctrine of believers being able to create whatever reality they verbalize, both good and bad, so we have to watch what we say.

The Deliverance and Spiritual-Warfare Movement

This movement teaches that committing sin opens doors and even gives authority to the Enemy to come into our lives. While that is true to some extent, the movement takes that idea further than the Bible does and interprets everything in terms of the influence of spirits, even things that might just be natural occurrences. In other words, this movement promotes hyper-spiritualization. Here are some things proponents of this movement claim to be gateways of demonic possession and oppression:

> Destruction is the action or process of destroying something. Curses open the door for the spirit of destruction (Osmodeus) to work with other spirits to destroy certain areas of an individual's life.

- Destruction of the mind (spirits of mental illness, schizo-phrenia, insanity, madness, confusion)
- Destruction of the finances (spirits of poverty, lack, debt, financial failure)
- Destruction of the body (spirits of sickness, infirmity, disease, plagues)
- Destruction of the marriage (spirits of Ahab, Jezebel, arguing, fighting, separation, divorce)
- Destruction of the family (spirits of death, accidents, rebellion, alcohol, strife, Ahab, Jezebel)[11]

Without going into the extensiveness of this movement's the-ology, it asserts that a sinful life leads to curses and gives the Enemy the legal right to destroy us. I do believe there are territorial spirits (see Deuteronomy 32:8–9; Psalm 82); however, I think it is im-portant that we not jump to the conclusion that everything that happens is due to the influence of spirits—that poverty, sickness, mental illness, and lust are all products of the reign of territorial spirits. As a result, this movement teaches that we have to use our spiritual authority to remove these things. Seeing something like poverty as an evil spirit means that our financial state is not a stewardship issue but a spiritual-warfare one.

What do these four movements have to do with rebranding pur-pose and dreaming? Embedded in the movements is a theology called dominion theology.

Dominion theology is the teaching that Christians are to take control over all areas of the secular realm: media, government, schools, arts, etc. It is also known as Christian reconstruction-ism and is often associated with theonomy—the rule of God in society.[12]

Theonomists interpret Genesis 1:26–28, where Adam and Eve were encouraged to subdue the earth, to mean that this is our destiny now. They believe that after the Fall, human beings surrendered dominion of the world to Satan. However, through the Cross and Resurrection, Jesus restored this dominion to Christians who now rule over everything Satan previously controlled. Dominion theology tells us that our main purpose is to take back media, government, and schools in the name of Jesus. This theology has had a deep effect on how many view money, purpose, and our control over our lives; it's made its way into several sectors of Western Christianity.

THE PURPOSE-DRIVEN LIFE

Rick Warren wrote one of the bestselling books of all time, *The Purpose Driven Life*, which has sold approximately fifty million copies. It has had an outstanding global impact, but many people took that book to a place Warren didn't intend; they made his book about personal purpose versus a larger divine purpose.

> It's not about you.
>
> The purpose of your life is far greater than your own personal fulfillment, your peace of mind, or even your happiness. It's far greater than your family, your career, or even your wildest dreams and ambitions. If you want to know why you were placed on this planet, you must begin with God. You were born by his purpose and for his purpose.[13]

That statement is the very focus of this chapter, but I want to broaden it. The only purpose worth living for is God's glory, not mine or yours. When we realize that, our lives will be better for it. The Bible says that God authors and finishes and perfects our faith (see Hebrews 12:1–3). It also says that He is the one who began a good work in us and that He will bring that work in us to completion (see Philippians 1:6). In addition, it says that we are His master work of art (see Ephesians 2:10). If these things are so, why wouldn't I trust the Manufacturer? In the Old Testament, it says, "Many plans are in a person's heart, but the LORD's decree will prevail" (Proverbs 19:21), which basically means that "human beings should plan for the future, but they should do so with the awareness that their plans may be overridden by God's purpose. Such an attitude engenders humility."[14] Bible interpreters suggest that "the point of the proverb is that the human being with many plans is uncertain, but the LORD with a sure plan gives correct counsel."[15] My favorite psalm is "The steps of a *good* man are ordered by the LORD" (37:23, KJV). God doesn't want us wandering in the darkness; He longs to guide us on our journey with Him.

The seeker-sensitive movement sought to build a bridge between the church and the lost by developing common ground with them. Many among the seeker-sensitive movement have helped the church to think about the lost again. I believe that was a good thing. The Gospel Coalition has an article called "Five Things the Seeker Movement Got Right," with the "five things" being the following:

- The Emphasis on Every Member Ministry
- An Emphasis on Community Through Relational Groupings
- An Incarnational Rethinking of Evangelism
- A Recovery of the Value of the Arts
- An Insistence That Faith Is for All of Life[16]

Those are significant benefits, and I can say that my church has been helped by each. However, the challenge has been that they aided the church in developing a consumeristic relationship with both non-Christians and Christians—an exchange of services for resources and attendance. Many churches became missiological on the surface but lacked depth and ultimately failed to help people grow in their souls. With that happening, some in the seeker-sensitive movement began to unintentionally brand the church and God as existing merely for us and not the other way around. This has created a substandard view of ecclesiology and disciple making.

What does all this have to do with purpose and dreaming? Everything! When you believe that purpose revolves around you and not the Lord and His kingdom, you create life goals that may not reflect the heart of God. Take a moment to consider one step you could take to center your life—your friendships, your work, your efforts to love and serve your family—on God's glory rather than your own. If we hope to rebrand the church for His glory, we need to start by acknowledging where we have failed to understand the assignment. The purpose of the church is to glorify God by making disciples. Rebranding the church requires us to carefully construct our hearts and lives around this purpose.

PURPOSE VERSUS ASSIGNMENT

Sermons about purpose and dreaming have done a lot of damage to our understanding of the church. People see their assignment, dream, gift, or talent as their purpose, and that's not fully biblical or true. Those things can serve biblical purposes, but they aren't core purposes themselves.

Let's define *purpose*. Purpose means functioning in our God-ordained design on the earth to the glory of God. I see purpose as less a specific season and more a constant movement of walking in the will of God. Purpose flows from who we are, not what we do. Walking in our purpose means growing to live more like Jesus and displaying Him to others. Purpose and calling are different yet connected. Purpose is the universal function of all believers; calling is the specific design given to someone to contribute to the purposes of God.

How does the Bible define purpose? In the Old Testament, there are a number of words that translate to *purpose*. Here are a few verses and definitions. "May he give you what your heart desires and fulfill your whole purpose" (Psalm 20:4). "The Hebrew word here is *asat*, meaning plan, scheme, and purpose—that is, to think about a course of action, often including consultation with a counselor or advisor."[17] Another verse says, "The reflections of the heart belong to mankind, but the answer of the tongue is from the LORD" (Proverbs 16:1). The word here for *reflections* is the Hebrew word that often translates as *purpose* or *plans*. It's the word "*ma'arak*, meaning plans and considerations—that is, an orderly, purposed arrangement of ideas with regard to future actions."[18] These verses illustrate how our personal plans connect with God's desired ends. Many times, we make our plans and desires our purpose; however, He measures our plans based on their connection to His desired ends.

Many people misappropriate the scripture that says, "Delight yourself in the LORD; and He will give you the desires of your heart" (Psalm 37:4, NASB). Most see it as God's serving our interests, meaning that if I worship, give, pray, get in the Word, and go to church, God will reward me with what I want. But nothing could be further from the truth. When we delight ourselves in the Lord, He begins to transform our desires. We begin to pray His will back to Him, and then He releases what He already wanted to do into our lives. Prayer, when rightly understood, isn't merely a dictation of our wills to God; it's alignment of our wills with His. God's will is known in principle in the Bible, but we tend to seek specific things in specific ways so that we can feel like we hit the bull's-eye in relationship to the King. Our motivation may be admirable, but our methods are often unbiblical.

God's will and purpose in our lives are a circle instead of a dot. In the garden, God said, "You are free to eat from any tree of the garden, but you must not eat from the tree of the knowledge of good and evil, for on the day you eat from it, you will certainly die" (Genesis 2:16–17). Adam and Eve had a plethora of trees to eat from in the garden. In addition, they could plant new ones and enjoy them as well. In the previous chapter of Genesis, it said, "God blessed them, and God said to them, 'Be fruitful, multiply, fill the earth, and subdue it'" (1:28). God placed people in the world. Humankind is not viewed as having an adversarial relationship with the world. The general meaning of the Hebrew verb *kabash* (כָּבַשׁ), translated "subdue" in Genesis 1:28, appears to be "to bring under one's control for one's advantage."[19] One might paraphrase the concept of subduing the earth as follows: "Harness its potential and use its resources for your benefit." In an ancient Israelite context, that would suggest cultivating its fields, mining its mineral riches, using its trees for construction, and domesticating its animals responsibly, in a way that promotes human flourishing for present and future generations.[20]

God's will is a larger pot than we think. For instance, many of us view marriage as finding the person who was made perfectly for you, almost like God betrothed you to someone from your birth. Conversely, the Bible seems to reflect more of a process of choosing wisely (see 1 Corinthians 7:39). Later on, Paul talks about choosing to remain single despite his rights as a believer and apostle: "Don't we have the right to be accompanied by a believing wife like the other apostles, the Lord's brothers, and Cephas?" (9:5). This verse indicates that choosing a spouse isn't about finding the exact combination to unlock your romantic destiny; it's about partnering with a person who's been regenerated. In other words, I think single believers are free to marry any person of the opposite sex who has a genuine relationship with Jesus Christ. According to the Bible, that relationship with the Lord is a fundamental requirement. Of course, we can have personal preferences, but we should be careful not to let those preferences override clear biblical principles.

THE PURPOSES OF GOD

God has larger purposes in the world than we tend to recognize. He has a vision for every aspect of His creation. Colossians 1:16 says,

> Everything was created by him,
> in heaven and on earth,
> the visible and the invisible,
> whether thrones or dominions
> or rulers or authorities—
> all things have been created through him and for him.

Specifically, Paul is talking about God the Son, the Lord Jesus the Christ. He is describing Jesus as the creator of the universe. In saying this, the apostle states that all things have been created through Him and for Him—that is, He is the means of creating all things, and all things He created possess an assigned purpose. The question is, What is His assigned purpose for us?

God's being in control doesn't mean He causes everything; it means that He will accomplish His desired ends despite the actions of His creation seen and unseen. We have God's directive will and His permissive will. His directive will is where He providentially and sovereignly brings about certain instances to execute His plan. For instance, the Bible says that Jesus Christ was slain before the foundations of the earth. When He causes the downfall of Egypt or the destruction of Jerusalem, His permissive will is using secondary means in light of man's lack of cooperation with His directive will. When people sin, it doesn't stop God's decrees. He is able to work our messes for His glory. One example is Laban's taking advantage of Jacob's work by giving him Leah instead of Rachel and then Jacob having to wait seven years to be able to marry Rachel. Out of all that sin and messiness and hurt, the Lord brought forth a nation of people. Sinful acts do not frustrate the plan of God, nor is He the author of them.

There are many purposes of God that are reflected in His divine decrees. Here, we will engage a few.

Self-Glorification

God's desire is communicated in the Westminster Confession of Faith, where it says, "The chief end of man is to glorify God and enjoy Him forever." At the end of the day, God is about God. I know that sounds selfish, but it isn't. His focus on Himself is to our benefit. His love for Himself drives Him to love and save humanity because both are in His nature. Peter says, "His divine power has granted to us everything pertaining to life and godliness, through the true knowledge of Him who called us by His own glory and excellence" (2 Peter 1:3, NASB). God called us by His own glory. He called us in response to Himself. His eternal enjoyment of Himself drove Him to create humankind and the world. In that drive, He desires that we pursue His glory. He is consumed by His own glory.

God chose his people for his glory:

He chose us in Him before the foundation of the world, that we would be holy and blameless before Him. In love He predestined us to adoption as sons through Jesus Christ to Himself, according to the kind intention of His will, to the praise of the glory of His grace. (Ephesians 1:4–6, NASB)

God created us for his glory:

Bring my sons from afar and my daughters from the end of the earth, everyone who is called by my name, whom I created for my glory. (Isaiah 43:6–7, ESV)

God raised Pharaoh up to show his power and glorify his name:

For the Scripture says to Pharaoh, "For this very purpose I have raised you up, that I might show my power in you, and that my name might be proclaimed in all the earth." (Romans 9:17, ESV)

For the glory of his name, God did not cast away his people:

Do not be afraid; you have done all this evil. Yet do not turn aside from following the LORD. . . . For the LORD will not forsake his people, for his great name's sake. (1 Samuel 12:20, 22, ESV)

Jesus endured his final hours of suffering for God's glory:

"Now is my soul troubled. And what shall I say? 'Father, save me from this hour?' But for this purpose I have come to this hour. Father, glorify your name." Then a voice came from heaven: "I have glorified it, and I will glorify it again." (John 12:27–28, ESV)

The ministry of the Holy Spirit is to glorify the Son of God:

He will glorify me, for he will take what is mine and declare it
to you. (John 16:14, ESV)[21]

Because God is motivated by His glory, we must be as well. His
glory is fundamental to our calling and purpose. Recall God's
command in Genesis 1:28 to "be fruitful, multiply"—God is
making clear that people are reflectors of His glory filling the
earth. That is why, according to the Great Commission, we are to
go to all the nations with the gospel (see Matthew 28:18–20).
We are to reflect God's glory for the purpose of helping others
see His glory and join us in the mission of reflecting His glory to
the world. We are to be reflectors, not robbers, because God
shares His glory with no one: "I am the LORD. That is my name,
and I will not give my glory to another or my praise to idols"
(Isaiah 42:8). "I will act for my own sake, indeed, my own, for
how can I be defiled? I will not give my glory to another" (48:11).
Our purpose is to glorify God, so when it comes to work, finances, relationships, business, community, resources, family,
parenting, singleness, and marriage, all these things are to be assignments that glorify God. Like Paul says, "Whether you eat or
drink, or whatever you do, do everything for the glory of God"
(1 Corinthians 10:31).

RESTORING AND CREATING IMAGE BEARERS

We have spoken much already on disciple making. Central to
God's purposes in the world is to saturate the earth with His glory
through the proclamation of the gospel and people becoming
mobile tabernacles of God's presence in the earth. Christ is said
to be the first human tabernacle: "The Word became flesh and
dwelt among us. We observed his glory, the glory as the one and
only Son from the Father, full of grace and truth" (John 1:14).

Craig Keener notes, "Like Moses of old (see 2 Cor 3:6–18), the disciples saw God's glory, now revealed in Jesus. As the Gospel unfolds, Jesus' glory is revealed in his signs (e.g., Jn 2:11) but especially in the cross, his ultimate act of love . . . (12:23–33). The Jewish people were expecting God to reveal his glory in something like a cosmic spectacle of fireworks."[22] John makes clear that the Word "did not merely manifest itself as an apparition; it literally became flesh."[23] We are examples of the presence of God on the earth. The church is His manifest presence by the power of the Holy Spirit through the gospel.

What if our churches' fundamental premise was people meeting Jesus in the gospel and growing to look like Him? If that were at the heart of all we do and say as the church, how might things be different? How might such a focus change our attitude about the church? How might it change the way the world sees us? Scripture tells us that "those [God] foreknew he also predestined to be conformed to the image of his Son" (Romans 8:29). Before we came into existence, it was the goal of God that we look like Jesus. God is constantly at work in the lives of believers to help them be more like Jesus. We should dedicate ourselves to doing everything for God's glory, from the most mundane to the most massive. And our personal goal in our every endeavor should be to be transformed into the image of Jesus, whether waiting in long lines or experiencing relationship drama, church hurt, financial trials, divorce, or sickness. All of it is used to work out our salvation. We need preachers and teachers who preach the whole counsel of God, not merely the parts that make us feel good. We must both encourage and rebuke. It should also be a community project of our encouraging one another with God's desired ends.

How will you devote yourself to His glory? How might your daily life need to change for it to be your focus? How might your calendar need to change for you to focus your life on God's glory?

How might your daily routines need to change to make growing in Christlikeness your priority? Take some time to give careful consideration to those questions. That is how we join in the work of rebranding the church for the glory of God and the good of the world.

7

REBRANDING THE CHURCH'S RELATIONSHIP WITH MEN

CHURCHES, NO MATTER THEIR ETHNIC MAKEUP, ARE USUALLY MADE up of more than 50 percent women. In the black community, sometimes the ratio seems to be even more lopsided. I have read countless resources on this and heard various reasons as to why it is the case. Most people seem to think it is due to sociological issues. In the beginning of our church, we were fifty-fifty. Later, it became almost 70 percent women and 30 percent men. Now we are creeping back to the 50 percent mark. When I began to notice that more women than men were present, I did not just stand idly by; as a leader, I voiced my desire to grow our male population through healthy gospel engagement. At the same time, we worked hard to make sure our sisters still knew they were deeply valued. It turned out that many of them had the same concerns.

I want us to see this chapter as a working document rather than set-in-stone principles that all should follow. More so, I hope Christian men can begin to have conversations about this issue and get to the bottom of it and even be part of the solution: to reach and disciple more men for Christ.

The relationship between men and church over the years has been complex, particularly for black men. It wasn't always that way. Many of the stats on our community are based on observation and not hard facts, as there isn't much data on the subject. From observing my church and talking to dozens of pastor friends, it is clear that there is a crisis surrounding black men's relationship with the church today.

There are many factors. Often, black men see the church as overly emotional, irrelevant, not engaging the community, geared more toward women, too wrapped up in the pastor, anti-intellectual, and morally bankrupt.

In 1913 in Chicago, Noble Drew Ali started the Moorish Science Temple of America (MSTA). Without going through much of their history, the Moors fundamentally desired that we African Americans realize we are actually Moors. The MSTA rejects the terms black, Negro, colored, and African American. Moors contend that black people were of North African origin and ruled Spain from 711 to 1492. Ali wanted black people to develop their own state and nation, so to speak. One of their statements says, "ALI'S MEN is dedicated to the uniting of the MSTA, and Operation Proclamation/the New Era Party is an organizing platform to bring Moorish America back together as a singular, unified political community."[1]

Fard and Elijah Muhammad, leaders of the Nation of Islam (NOI), studied Ali's teachings but created another, even more radical entity.[2] They became more radical in their view of race, Christianity, the church, men, and women. One of the sacred texts of the NOI is the message to the black man. Fard and Elijah believed that if they could reach the men, they would reach the rest of the family as well. Their mission field for recruitment was the streets, the jails, and the black church. Their main goal was to put black men in opposition to the church by framing the church as an enemy and its leaders as liars. Most Black Religious Identity Cults (BRICs) adopted much of the NOI's ideologies and mission fields. Here are a few statements from Elijah Muhammad:

> The greatest hindrance to the truth of our people is the preacher of Christianity. He will not accept it, nor is he content to let others alone who are trying to accept the truth. He is the man who stands in the way of the salvation of his people, and as soon as the people awaken to the knowledge of this man in their way to God, freedom, justice and equality and stop following him, the sooner they will be in heaven while they live. . . .
>
> Our first step is to give back to the white man his religion (Christianity), his church, and his names. These three are chains of slavery that hold us in bondage to them. We are free when we give up the above three.[3]

For the past hundred years, these groups, with the NOI as the forerunner, have sought to deter men from finding Christianity, the church, and the gospel. From Malcolm X to Farrakhan, they have denounced Christianity as a relevant option for black men. In the 1960s, Clarence 13X, a former member of the NOI, started the Five Percent Nation of Islam. They believed that 85 percent of the world is blind, 10 percent know the truth and don't do anything about it, and they are the 5 percent who know and do. The Five Percent Nation has successfully recruited many hip-hop celebrities, including Rakim, Big Daddy Kane, Jay-Z, Busta Rhymes, Wu-Tang Clan, and Poor Righteous Teachers. These voices did a number on the image of the church, Christianity, and black identity. Each of the groups view the church as the enemy of Christianity. The internet has expanded their influence; even if a person didn't join these groups, their sentiments on things such as justice, race, economics, identity, and Christianity had a strong influence on many black men.

Other factors souring black men toward the church include blaxploitation films and shows, church hurt, immorality in the pulpit, the extravagant and immodest lifestyles of pastors, lack of cultural and community engagement, and church scandals.

It should also be mentioned that after the civil rights movement, the church began to decline as a central institution in the black community. As the world became less segregated, institutions previously closed off to black people began to open up. As a result, many black people became less reliant on the church for social engagement and change.

One thing to note is that most BRICs intentionally go after men as their first and central mission field. Although I think BRICs are deeply problematic, I admire the way they engage men where they are rather than waiting for men to come to them. I strongly believe we can learn from them in that regard.

The Great Migration was the height of the black church's influence in the black community in urban centers.

> However, during the migrations there was no evidence of a great decline in church membership in urban areas. In fact, the majority of black migrants did not abandon their churches, but continued to seek refuge, help, fellowship, and collective community efforts in the confines of the only institution they had known. If they did not feel comfortable in the large established black churches, they helped create smaller ones by first meeting in homes, then renting storefronts, and later purchasing their own church edifices. Black preachers attracted people by their personal charisma and ability to preach and lead, and sometimes by their moral charisma of earnestness and hard work. In

less than a century a largely rural population had been trans-formed into an urban one.[4]

Prior to the civil rights movement, the black family was con-nected and strong. Not long after that movement, there was the welfare era. One of the unintended results of welfare was the separation of the black man from the black woman. That deeply affected the church's relationship with the black family and caused black children in the welfare system to be more likely to have members of their family investigated by Child Protective Services and their parents' rights terminated.

> [A] history of punitive regulations has dogged social welfare policy. A classic example of this is the "man in the house" rule enforced throughout the 1960s. . . . [which] prevented adult males from residing with mothers and children who received assistance. . . . [These rules] enforced through highly invasive inspections, forced many families to choose between maintain-ing welfare supports and keeping their families intact.[5]

When that happened, in many places, ministry outreach to fam-ilies focused primarily on women and not the whole family unit. In many ways, this played a pivotal role in how church was contextual-ized for women and children to the neglect of men. Sociologist Elijah Anderson communicates this impact on the family well:

> Some working poor people survive by living with kin and thus sharing household duties and close family life—joys as well as troubles. A large number of the women are on welfare, and many are very apprehensive about "welfare reform." Eligible men seem a scarce presence in their lives.

> When present at all, men appear most often in the roles of nephew, cousin, father, uncle, boyfriend, and son, but seldom as husband.[6]

The absence of a stable husband in the home sets a precedent in a community that is filled with thousands of single mothers and very few married couples. In the midst of the loss of many things for the black family, this situation may contribute to men becoming disconnected from the church, while women often assume the role of spiritual leaders within many families.

THE CHURCH'S ROLE IN FAILING TO REACH AND RETAIN MEN

We've established that the church is struggling to reach men, and that brings up the question of why. There are many reasons I will unpack shortly, but let's start with one of the reasons many men have a hard time taking the church seriously. I think we often assume that men don't want to go to church because they think it's boring or irrelevant. Although some men certainly feel that way, I also think there are many men out there who hear stories of pastors and other church leaders living deeply hypocritical lifestyles.

Lower Standards for Pastoral Maturity

When pastors' actions go viral, it's not typically for good reasons. What goes viral is not the sound teaching of the Word but rather foolishness and buffoonery: extravagant clothing, multiple offertories, spiritual abuse, manipulation, inauthenticity, cursing, irrational thinking, and bad theology. So many YouTube channels and social media platforms are built around how bad the pulpit has gotten. I'm not a fan of those channels, but we must admit that there is too much fodder in the wild. I've seen some crazy stuff out there—encouraging the church to grow drugs to attract men, the mismanagement of communion, womanizing, and just plain old unwise leadership. Christian YouTuber Ruslan KD has said that many pastors today are influencers, not shepherds.[7] I wholeheartedly agree.

The amount of moral compromise that is normalized in our churches is heartbreaking. Church leaders bring in known whoremongers to preach in their churches. There is a culture in some church circles where pastors are just out there living their best lives, including having affairs and misusing their churches' money. People know and whisper about it yet still happily attend events where these immoral leaders preach. Because these pastors are good communicators whose preaching draws a crowd, no one says anything. I understand and even empathize with someone who falls and goes through a restoration process to get healthy and restored to ministry; however, this indifference toward sexual immorality is scary. It scares me that someone can get with a woman and even other men on a regular basis and then preach on Sunday as if nothing ever happened. Congregations know that their leaders are morally corrupt, but they do nothing about it. As a result, the expectations of leadership and the standard of holiness at the church drop. This reminds me of a story in the Bible.

Eli's sons were wicked, and he was passive in dealing with their sin:

> Eli was very old; and he heard all that his sons were doing to all Israel, and how they lay with the women who served at the doorway of the tent of meeting. He said to them, "Why do you do such things, the evil things that I hear from all these people? No, my sons; for the report is not good which I hear the LORD's people circulating. If one man sins against another, God will mediate for him; but if a man sins against the LORD, who can

intercede for him?" But they would not listen to the voice of their father, for the LORD desired to put them to death. (1 Samuel 2:22–25, NASB)

Prior to the temple being built, the "tent of meeting" was "where the Lord appeared to his people and their leaders."[8] Eli's sons had no respect for the presence of the Lord. The women were there to serve the Lord, not their sexual appetites. We live in a world where some churches are the family business. Some of these churches have developed cultures where the congregation is viewed as serving the desires and needs of the leadership, rather than leaders seeing themselves as serving God and His people. I am not arguing that shepherds shouldn't be compensated well; what I am concerned about is an absolute abuse of power. One church had such deep nepotism that the pastor placed his son as his successor despite the fact that the younger man was not qualified. Many of the family members were on staff, and it was more of a family move than a kingdom one.

Scripture doesn't mince words when it comes to false teachers. False teachers and false prophets aren't just those who preach heresy and heterodoxy; they are also those who have false lives that are fully committed to sin with no conviction of the Spirit. John says, "If we say that we have fellowship with Him and yet walk in the darkness, we lie and do not practice the truth" (1 John 1:6, NASB). He is talking about a life of comprehensive willful sin. The idea here is to have an affinity toward darkness. Paul also talks about the damaging effects of allowing publicly known sin to go unchecked as we saw earlier in 1 Corinthians 5:6. In other words, what's good in the church can be contaminated by not discipling people or by failing to uphold standards of holiness or address the mess in the church. He then says, "Clean out the old leaven so that you may be a new unleavened batch, as indeed you are. For Christ our Passover lamb has been sacrificed" (1 Corinthians 5:7).

The lack of discipleship and accountability has had an adverse effect on men and their view of the church. Unchecked sin can have a leavening effect, spreading throughout other areas of the church and into the lives of others, causing more and more damage. A person's rampant sin doesn't just produce the same sin but rather a pandemic of sin. Like yeast in bread, it will permeate the whole lump. Apathy sets in, moral authority is lost, and the holiness of God isn't taken seriously. Statements like "You can't judge," "Nobody's perfect," and "Let he without sin cast the first stone" often become slogans and anthems not only of those caught in sin but of the church as a whole. That leads to a spiritually immature church at best and a savagely ungodly church at worst—what John would call "a love-abandoned church" (see Revelation 2:4–5).

Preaching That Caters to Women

I was recently perusing sermon clips on Instagram and in a short span, I came across at least ten sermons that made women's issues the fault of men. It was either the fault of the father, brother, boyfriend, or husband. It all starts with, "That man hurt you, but God is about to do_____ on your behalf!" After that the church goes ballistic. I just think it's low-hanging fruit in order to get a response.

One of the things I like about the current generation of men who are millennials or Gen Z is they are hungry for engagement, intellectually and spiritually. More than ever, men are open to theological dialogue. Most of the time, they want explanation. Another example of how Black Religious Identity Cults are successful is that they aren't afraid to get on the front lines of the streets and online to engage men. I am encouraged to see that happening more and more among male believers, but it needs to increase and be part of our evangelism strategy for men.

Money-Centeredness

When churches have multiple offertories and use false prophesies to manipulate giving, it is a major turnoff for many men. The Bible says that greed is often a sign of a false teacher. According to Peter, this is how false teachers operate: "They will exploit you in their greed with made-up stories. Their condemnation, pronounced long ago, is not idle, and their destruction does not sleep" (2 Peter 2:3). "The term 'greed' (*pleonexia* [also in 2:14]) could be a reference to the lust for power, food, sex, or financial gain."[9] Peter goes on to say, "They have eyes full of adultery that never stop looking for sin. They seduce unstable people and have hearts trained in greed. Children under a curse!" (verse 14). False prophets and teachers use people's desire for money to trap them for their own personal gain while leaving their victims bankrupt financially and spiritually. Men wisely have peeped the game of these pulpit pimps. Many have noticed the pattern of false teachers producing content about money rather than soul engagement and helping change the world. The only problem is that all preachers end up being branded in the same way as these false teachers. Many of us are trying to change this narrative.

I tell people all the time that money-centered churches are not the norm. Not one of my preacher friends got in this field for the money. Many are underpaid and don't have insurance or retirement. Most pastors I know would do this work for free. That is why believers need to post video clips of solid preachers and teachers who address this very subject. There are already some doing so on TikTok and Instagram. In the comments, people often say, "We need to hear more preaching like this." When that happens, it is a kingdom win because rebranding starts with re-presenting.

CORE CULTURAL CONCERNS

Some of the core cultural concerns of black men are survival, refuge, and resistance to oppression. Others would be human dignity, African identity, the divine significance of the African American experience, and economic solidarity. Although the black church has done a lot for black communities, there arose this sense in the black community, even today, that the church is responsible for solving our communities' economic problems, family issues, educational challenges, and housing realities. Many make the point that if the church isn't doing those things, the church isn't needed.

I believe in the church investing in the community, but our primary mission isn't community development; it's eternal soul development. An outworking of the gospel can be contextual community development. As stated in Titus 3:14, our people must also learn to engage in good deeds to meet "pressing needs, so that they will not be unfruitful." We will explore that more in our chapter on outreach and evangelism. Not everything is the church's fault, yet we must own what we must on all fronts, including the walls we may have put up between the church and black men.

We need more men to step up and help solve the problem of declining male engagement at church and help one another address the core cultural concerns of men. For instance, we had an entrepreneurial expo at our church that was led by young men in our church. They identified some core needs of men and structured the expo around those needs. When we make the effort to understand them, men show up in force, particularly to our conference events. In our context, this includes demonstrating a working understanding of justice issues and black identity. We strive to infuse these understandings into our church ministry as a whole and men's ministry in particular. I believe that having a men's ministry is essential, but we need more than men's breakfasts. I think our churches need teams of men committed to contextualizing and meeting the unique needs of men. The sisters can encourage men in the church in that as well. I love when the members of my church get passionate and want to implement a new initiative to meet a need. I encourage such members to develop a proposal with their objectives and goals demonstrating how their initiative or program plugs into the church's overall vision and mission.

So, if you are a church leader, don't feel as though the impetus to reach men falls solely on your shoulders. Embrace the passion of others in your church who want to help, and empower them to get to work. I would also encourage you not to be overprotective of the programs your church already offers. Honestly assess them. If they are failing to reach men, then perhaps it is time to humbly reconsider your approach. None of your church's programs should be too precious to be changed or recontextualized.

If you are not in church leadership but have a passion for helping your church reach men, maybe it is time for you to step up and start doing so. Put together a plan with a clear vision and goals that connect to your church's overall mission and values, and present that to the leaders of your church. Don't be overbearing and demand they get on board, but humbly offer yourself as someone who wants to help the church reach men. Most healthy leaders would welcome such engagement, but the pastoral leadership must champion the cause in order for it to be effective and a priority.

ENGAGING MEN IN HEALTHY WAYS

Discipleship is the flagship mechanism the whole church needs. Approaching men to be disciples is a must. Men must be sought after. Most aren't keen on asking to be pulled in close. When I say "pulled in close," I'm talking about serving, learning, accountability, and life-on-life engagement. Start with the men in your church who are willing—who have expressed a desire to grow and serve. At my church, we have sought to make clear what a disciple is and what the means of discipleship are. When people try to give me a syllabus of what they want, I push back and tell them what is available for their growth already. I don't babysit people, but at some points, I meet them where they are so they may go beyond where they are. For men, discipleship must be organized and organic. By *organized*, I mean there are classes and times of clear engagement. Everything we do in the church should contribute to discipleship: Sunday morning services, equipping events, small groups, men's time, men's retreats, men's outings, service projects, serving, and investing in others. By *organic*, I mean committing to doing things without the church having organized it. When people organically take responsibility for the mission of Christ in the world, it brings great fruit. Let me explain. Key men open their homes, lock arms with men that need engagement, and just chill together or go through resources together. In our men's ministry, we have men's smaller groups or pods where they connect, encourage, and hold one another accountable. It's refreshing for them. We have a leadership team of men in charge of leading other men through the process and building community. Men go golfing and to the shooting range, engage in Christian liberties with self-control, and much more. They bond deep.

LEARNING THE FAITH

Men don't like to be caught off guard. They love to be thorough in whatever they are part of. In my experience, men want to be taught! All the extra programs churches offer are cool, but teaching the Word is crucial. Teaching the Bible may or may not draw a crowd, but it will grow men. Our church is currently about 50 percent men. The main thing I hear from men as to what attracted them to our church is faithful, clear preaching and teaching of the Bible. It is very hard for men to trust, and sound teaching of the Word—not only communicating soundly but also functioning under that Word soundly—is one of the most powerful means for building that trust. When men know that the church is committed to the Word of Christ, it builds credibility.

What it boils down to is this: Don't settle. Go where you can be challenged. It's good for a ministry to meet you where you are, but we need ministers who push us beyond where we are into who God wants us to be. You need to be part of a church that deliberately challenges you to be more like Jesus (see Hebrews 6:1–2).

CREATING A SAFE PLACE TO BE BROKEN AND HEALED

Men need a safe environment where they can work through life. They need family, companionship, friendship, and community. Women naturally connect with women, but men need a bit of a runway to build relationships and trust. That is why men in the body of the church must become a safe place for other brothers in Christ, so let's take a moment to talk about mental health.

Mental health issues often barricade men from being emotionally available to their wives, families, children, friends, and gospel communities. Whether we have just ended a serious relationship or are coping with family issues, being emotionally available is a state of mind that ebbs and flows. It plays a major role in determining whether or not a relationship will blossom. If one person in a pair isn't able to connect with the other person emotionally, intimacy can't grow. "To say a person is emotionally available means being present in a way that goes beyond physical proximity," explains psychologist Joel Frank. "It's about being open to truly understand, empathize, and reciprocate the emotions of others. It refers to our ability to share an emotional connection with others and to be open to receiving their emotions in return."[10]

Men, you have to be developed by the church and the family to grow toward emotional maturity. Why is that important? Because Scripture tells us that devoting our lives to God requires us to grow in empathy toward others:

> Share with the saints in their needs; pursue hospitality. Bless those who persecute you; bless and do not curse. Rejoice with those who rejoice; weep with those who weep. Live in harmony with one another. Do not be proud; instead, associate with the humble. Do not be wise in your own estimation. Do not repay anyone evil for evil. Give careful thought to do what is honorable in everyone's eyes. (Romans 12:13–17)

Every follower of Christ has been given the capacity, through our new life in Jesus, to be empathetic in very practical ways. You may not always know how to support someone else's mental health, but faith in Christ empowers us to be kind, emotionally intelligent people who can, at the very least, be supportive of one another's growth.

I should give a shout-out to the millennials in my church because they have essentially introduced therapy to our community and helped us get rid of the stigma of going to therapy. It is now safe for church members to say they are in therapy without people thinking about them a certain way or even judging our church. Even so, many men still avoid therapy, or if they go, they fail to open up about their wounds or acquire the tools needed to break the cycles that plague their lives. We have to own and take seriously our comprehensive health. We should see dealing with our mental health as men as part of our spiritual formation. Dealing with "daddy wounds," our environments growing up, molestation, and neglect must be handled with tremendous care so that we can show up for our families, ourselves, our church, and Jesus. When we deal with our wounds, it creates empathy for others because it opens us to seeing life better.

The ability to be empathetic takes emotional maturity. For more information on what emotional maturity looks like, I highly recommend Peter Scazzero's book *Emotionally Healthy Spirituality*. In it, he walks us through the process of maturing from being emotional infants to being emotionally healthy adults.[11]

Discipleship must include movement toward emotional maturity. While we should not expect the programs of our churches to take the place of therapy for those who need it, we must make sure our small groups understand God's grace in giving people space to grow and work through their struggles and issues. We need to understand that not every struggle is a sin issue. However, for clear sin issues, the church must be a safe place for learning how to confess and repent from sin. Far from competing with the church, therapy can work alongside the church and help us unearth anything that holds back our ability to emote in healthy ways.

A few years ago, I was in therapy. I had become exhausted and disconnected from my wife and very impatient. My therapist said that I had compassion fatigue.

Compassion fatigue involves emotional and physical exhaustion that can affect people who have been exposed to other people's traumas or stressors. It is characterized by a decreased ability to empathize, feelings of helplessness, and burnout due to the demands of supporting those who are suffering.[12]

Having been a caregiver to my wife for almost three decades and a provider and caregiver to my children in multiple capacities, I was just emotionally worn out. Additionally, dealing with so much church trauma and foolish things on my ministry platform left me with nothing more to give.

To the men reading this, I want to encourage you to plug into a local church with mature leadership. Strive to develop and foster healthy community by making yourself available to others in the body and, if needed, going to therapy. Intentionality is important. You have to take responsibility for your own wholeness. Those who are part of your tribe are there to encourage you and help you grow. Proverbs 18:1 talks about how when we isolate ourselves, we are being selfish and breaking out against all counsel. Being teachable takes humility and vulnerability. That doesn't mean you wear your heart on your sleeve, but it does mean that as you build safe places and relationships of trust, you let them be what God has brought them into your life for. That is why you have to pray for those things and seek them out.

MANHOOD DEFINED

In the current world we live in, there are a slew of podcasts on relationships, men, women, high-value men, and what women and men want from the opposite sex. The template many of these podcasts use is male personality types. By comparison, the Bible doesn't teach specific personality types for men or women. Scripture does describe people based on how their lives compare to virtues of holiness or to sin issues. For instance, Jesus describes Nathanael as someone who isn't deceitful (see John 1:47); He basically calls him a stand-up dude. On the other hand, a man named Diotrephes is spoken of differently: "I wrote something to the church, but Diotrephes, who loves to have first place among them, does not receive our authority" (3 John 1:9).

When asked "What is a man?" people come up with various definitions—some conflicting, some evolving, some toxic, and others traditional or patriarchal. Some people may snarl at the idea of biblical manhood or womanhood. However, in this fleeting culture that seeks to redefine what God has already given clear meaning to, we must be clear as believers, and not just about gender but also about roles and function. A men's ministry called 33 The Series, formerly known as Men's Fraternity, gives what I think is a clear and biblically encapsulating definition of manhood: that men should accept responsibility, reject passivity, lead courageously, and invest eternally.[13] For us as believers, our wiring and personality types, real or perceived, don't exempt us as men from the biblical responsibilities God requires of all His people.

Men, it is time for us to make the most of what God has made available to us and be a means of encouragement for other men. Join me in actively rebranding our relationship with the church. We should no longer be the guys who go to church because a woman we like asked us to. We shouldn't be begged to pray and lead and serve. We should be the initiators of those things. The rebranding of our relationship with the church is happening, but we must cover more ground. We start by embracing our roles as active and engaged members of the kingdom of our Lord and Savior, Jesus Christ.

8

REBRANDING EVANGELISM AND MISSION

IN THE BLACK COMMUNITY, THERE IS AN ONGOING DIALOGUE ABOUT what the church does for black people. A few years ago, I was on BET with T.I., Talib Kweli, and two activists to discuss how the black church used to be at the forefront of black issues of justice, economics, and equality but is not so much anymore. The host, Angela Rye, asked me, "What is your church doing to impact your community and city?" It wasn't the prearranged question she was supposed to ask, so I nervously shared some of our actions and plans. Afterward, the panel and many of the audience members came up to talk to me. They seemed hungry for the church to get in the game on these issues in the world and our community.

There seems to be a strong cultural expectation today for the church, particularly in the black community, to be engaged in the world—for churches to be making a difference in their surrounding communities. Specifically in the black community, there is an expectation for the church to fix all kinds of social issues. To my knowledge, there isn't another people group that

places that level of responsibility on the church. I remember seeing a woman on a Black Lives Matter panel many years ago encouraging black people not to give to their church unless it is
doing work in the black community.[1] Many don't know the fundamental purpose of the church. I'm not saying there isn't a
point to be made of church involvement, but it seems many people are clueless to the central mission of the church.

Recently, on a popular podcast called *Hardly Initiated*, Umar John-
son, the self-proclaimed Prince of Pan-Africanism, stated that the
black church caters to the black woman and keeps her single in
order to get her to continue giving money to the church and stay
dependent on the church.[2] On *The Joe Budden Podcast*, Umar declared
that every black church should have a bank, a school, and a garden.[3]
He even pointed out that if the church has at least $250,000 in
yearly income, it should have those three things. First off, $250,000
is nowhere near enough to run a bank or school. Also, most
churches in underserved areas have fewer than fifty members.
Umar added that churches are just selling us hope and we get nothing in return. In the comments, many people agreed. In other
words, many in my community view the church as an investment
institution for the purpose of solving problems in the community.

I agree to an extent.

In our cities and beyond, the church at large has lost its missiological edge in numerous ways. Some are more focused on
being attractional than missiological, both traditional historic
churches and newer church plants. Others are known more for
what they are against than what they are for. And still others are
simply dying because they lack mission. Structures are falling
apart as an era has passed, and the city is changing in some ways
but also suffering from systemic problems. Many churches that
are still going have invested in and served their communities in
significant ways.

Exactly three blocks from the church I pastor is a historic church called Berean Presbyterian Church (BPC). This church still meets and operates, but it no longer has the institutions it had in the past. In his landmark work about my city, W.E.B. Du Bois points out that this institutional church was started, funded, and run primarily by black people. It had "a successful Building and Loan Association, a kindergarten, a medical dispensary and a seaside home, beside the numerous church societies."[4] He goes on to say, "Probably no church in the city, except the Episcopal Church of the Crucifixion, is doing so much for the social betterment of the Negro."[5] BPC established the Berean Building and Loan Association in 1888. The majority of its officers were black, and to illustrate its impact on the community, Du Bois said that "its income for 1896 was nearly $30,000, and it had $60,000 in loans; 43 homes have been bought through this association."[6]

Reverend Matthew Anderson of the historic BPC in Philly was a pioneer of his time. He started a bank for those affected by segregation and a trade school of sorts. So many other ministries and leaders during that period filled in where the times failed them, and those institutions bred many who would go on to be amazing citizens. Some became homeowners, and others started schools and businesses and organizations for the betterment of the community. I wonder whether today's church is still ripe for this type of institution building. People in the communities around our churches are asking for it, but will there be participation and engagement?

WE HAVE LOST OUR MISSIOLOGICAL EDGE

"Missiology is the study of the salvation activities of the Father, Son, and Holy Spirit throughout the world geared toward bringing the kingdom of God into existence."[7] "Evangelism is defined as sharing the good news of Christ's substitutionary death and resurrection and His free offer of forgiveness for sin and eternal life to all who, by faith, come to Him to receive it. Evangelism . . . is done with the clear intent of bringing the hearer to faith in Jesus Christ for salvation."[8]

Churches are dying at an alarming rate. Some are dying slowly, and others expeditiously. Thom Rainer gives six reasons why that is happening:

1. They refuse to admit they are sick, very sick.
2. They are still waiting on the "magic bullet" pastor.
3. They fail to accept responsibility.
4. They are not willing to change—at all.
5. Their "solutions" are all inwardly focused.
6. They desire to return to 1985.[9]

All those are true and compelling reasons; however, I'd like to address being inwardly focused. So many urban and even suburban places are rapidly growing and gentrifying. Considering the changing demographics, we should be committed to relearning our communities. Some of our churches need to make a transition of some sort. Too many churches see their surroundings as a threat rather than an opportunity. Some ministries cocoon themselves into their walls and die a slow and agonizing death. They think they are preserving what they built, but in reality, they are letting their churches decay.

A friend of mine in a large city is pastoring a historic church. Their neighborhood has drastically changed. Developers offered to buy their building for tens of millions of dollars and build them another. The church refuses to do so because they are more connected to what *was* than to what God can do *now*. Too many historic churches go up in flames wishing for an era that will never return. They refuse to believe God for new wind for a new season.

I have other pastor friends whose churches have become staples in their communities, cities, and now the world. The churches have grown in attendance and membership by leaps and bounds and have done innovative ministry, leading many to Christ. My friend Bryan Carter succeeded the late great Dr. E. K. Bailey at Concord Church in Dallas. Under Carter's leadership, the church has grown from three thousand to approximately twelve thousand members, with significant growth among the younger generations. His church didn't disconnect from the older generations either. He did some beautiful and Christlike things, including reaching out to couples from his church who were engaging in sex before marriage and offering them premarital counseling. Carter told them to take care of their relationship and that the church would take care of paying for the wedding. Simple acts like these demonstrated care and dramatically raised the church's estimation in the community.

THE FUNDAMENTAL PURPOSE OF THE CHURCH

The fundamental mission of the church is to make disciples (see Matthew 28:18–20). Making disciples merely means proclaiming the gospel to people and then helping those who believe to become healthy image bearers in every area of life. God is about the saving and shaping of the whole person: "May the God of peace himself sanctify you completely. And may your whole spirit, soul, and body be kept sound and blameless at the coming of our Lord Jesus Christ" (1 Thessalonians 5:23). Paul's "desire is that God will *sanctify you through and through*. . . . The current petition is that they may be sanctified *through and through*, or 'entirely,' so that they reach 'the full end or goal' for which they were saved."[10] The implied goal here is wholeness—that people would increasingly grow into their full image-bearing potential and that the gospel would shape every part of their beings. However, before people can be sanctified, they must be reached.

In the work to save the whole person, we are to engage people on every level. Our missions and outreach are means to show people the kingdom. God's desire is for people to experience His kingdom. Jesus's miracles were commercials for His coming rule. When Jesus was accused of casting out demons by the power of Beelzebul, He said, "If I drive out demons by Beelzebul, by whom do your sons drive them out? For this reason they will be your judges. If I drive out demons by the Spirit of God, then the kingdom of God has come upon you" (Matthew 12:27–28). The coming of the kingdom is to be discerned in Jesus's defeat of the demons. Mostly, Matthew speaks of the kingdom as the future, but here it is a present reality.[11]

Jesus expected us to live as commercials for the coming attraction of the kingdom. The Lord's outreach was a means to show people who He is and communicate and authenticate the message:

> When John heard in prison what the Christ was doing, he sent a message through his disciples and asked him, "Are you the one who is to come, or should we expect someone else?"
>
> Jesus replied to them, "Go and report to John what you hear and see: The blind receive their sight, the lame walk, those with leprosy are cleansed, the deaf hear, the dead are raised, and the poor are told the good news, and blessed is the one who isn't offended by me." (Matthew 11:2–6)

It's one thing to respond to the miracle, but it's another to put one's trust in the Miracle Worker. John was very strategic with how he used miracles in telling the good news about Jesus. The miracles that John, the eyewitness, chose to record in his gospel were carefully selected. In all seven miracles, or miraculous signs (as John preferred to call them), Jesus is seen as the Son of God. In addition, each miracle had something special to reveal.[12]

We must have contextual means of connecting. Many times, miracles come in the form of outreach in our communities. The type of kingdom Jesus established on earth tells us that God wants to be involved in every area of our lives. That is why we need a holistic gospel. Having the gospel touch every facet of our lives is important, and therefore our outreach must be a demonstration of the love and care of God to bring shalom to our communities and world. God's shalom is the means by which He stitches things back to the way He wants them to be. Our theology needs to be able to touch the block, the ground, and where people are. Some call this Christian community development:

> The gospel, rightly understood, is wholistic. It responds to people as whole people. . . . Christian community development begins with people transformed by the love of God, who then respond to God's call to share the gospel with others through evangelism, social action, economic development, and justice. These groups of Christians start both churches and community development corporations, evangelism outreaches and tutoring programs, discipleship groups and housing programs, prayer groups and businesses.[13]

Holistic and comprehensive are words that encapsulate the way the gospel works. The gospel has both a content and a scope. Tony Evans illustrates this well:

> We need to align our lives under an agenda that is a comprehensive demonstration of the way our Creator intended every area of life to be lived. An agenda big enough to include both indi-

viduals and societal structures, clear enough to be understood and appropriated by the average person on the street, yet flexible enough to allow for the considerable differences among peoples and societies.[14]

Whether we minister overseas or on our own soil, assessing differences is important. When our church started helping and supporting the work of churches and church plants in Malawi, Africa, we had to contextualize our efforts based on their unique needs as an entryway into church planting, leadership development, and outreach and evangelism. For example, young girls from a village in the capital city had to walk two to three hours daily to get to school. Many of them were accosted, molested, or raped on this journey. As a result, the leadership of the church asked us to help build a school in their section of the city. Once the school was built, a waiting list to attend it filled up quickly. The government of Malawi's capital, Lilongwe, heard what we were doing and built water lines out to that part of the country. For the first time, that area had a source of fresh water. For them, that was a massive miracle and answer to prayer. Through that and the tireless effort of Pastor Robert Manda and others, the gospel reached hundreds. Many chiefs came to Jesus, and they had access to and influence on hundreds of thousands more people. The gospel spread because it had been communicated and lived out simultaneously. From there, we were able to help support a residency program for many leaders who would plant churches.

All believers should see themselves as missionaries. As a follower of Jesus, your mission field includes the grocery store, the barbershop or beauty salon, parks, bars, the gym—basically, all places. You are a missionary. The role of the church is to equip, and every believer has a role in equipping, both in terms of seeking it out for themselves and participating in the equipping of others. Many churches say that every member is a minister; I'd add that every believer is a missionary and evangelist to some degree. At some point, the non-Christian people in your sphere of influence should hear the gospel from you. That is why Paul challenges the Colossians to build common ground with outsiders and seek opportunities to tell people about Jesus. When you go out to eat, you could just say to the server, "Is there any way we can be praying for you? We are about to say grace over the food." I can't tell you how many times servers have cried and shared reasons they needed prayer, which led to opportunities to share the gospel with them.

THE NEED TO EXEGETE OUR CITY

One of my favorite pastimes is to drive around cities and take in the architecture, people, business, food, art—whatever the city has to offer. Some of my favorite cities are DC, Philadelphia, Dallas, Chicago, and New York (in limited doses). My creative juices start flowing when I'm in those cities; I think about ministry and church planting. In my city, Philly, I pray while driving, walking, or bicycling. I observe how our neighborhood is faring. City stats don't really give a primary cultural view; it's only secondary cultural data. Most stats don't account for the particulars of black communities, such as who is nosy, who is helpful, where the drug houses are, what the best papi store is, who is reliable, and what the politics in the neighborhood are.

In every city, there are both visible and invisible systems. Visible systems are the obvious things: grocery stores, block captains, bus stops, train stations, and so on. Invisible systems are neighborhood boundaries, graffiti tags, where drugs can be bought, how to find out who stole something, and who can get the items back. When a building permit gets rejected for no good reason, understanding the invisible systems means you will know who can help get it approved. It's not just paperwork; it's people work. Our ministry was trying to buy a 133-thousand-square-foot school on several acres of land. We met with different stakeholders in the community and got approved on the local level, but when it went to the larger voting system, it got tabled at every meeting for several years. We eventually gave up. We later found out that this frustrating process was driven by internal politics. There is good and bad in both systems, but the church needs to have an incarnational ministry that can engage those systems to serve the city well and reach people.

I want to encourage you to be committed to making a difference. Don't let resistance keep you from dreaming and planning ways you can love and serve your community. Now is the time to dream, plan, and study ways you might build structures and initiatives that will promote the flourishing of the people in the neighborhoods around your church.

Every year, we hit the blocks in our community and ask people questions. We ask, "What are the three greatest influences in your community? What are the top three needs? And what can the church do to meet those needs?" Many times, people are astounded that we are even out there asking those kinds of questions. Often churches or leaders simply assume what the city needs and then wonder why there is a disconnect. Vision is never generated in a vacuum. Vision is never about a personal dream. It's about the practical entry points that build bridges to the gospel.

Your vision for ministry needs to be contextualized to the people in your community you are trying to reach. If you don't know the people in your community—their struggles and hopes, the problems they face, and the needs they feel on a regular basis—your vision for ministry is unlikely to connect with them.

Ask questions of the community around your church before engaging it. Churches should work hard at understanding their communities, as Mark Gornik points out:

> Whenever a church defines a community and its needs apart from the people of the community, a manipulative process is set in motion, one that often serves only the extension of the church's own interests, goals, and power. Language, agenda-setting, and unconsciously held notions of superiority are common conductors of a manipulative process.[15]

The late Harvie M. Conn and the late Manuel Ortiz, in their landmark work *Urban Ministry*, give three key categories that ministries should consider as they seek to reach their communities with the gospel: identification, engagement, and recording. The **identification** process involves singling out a geography and population in a particular part of a city or town. The goal is to both acquire census information and get out in the city to find out the real information about the neighborhood. Doing this leads us to the engagement process.

The second category, **engagement,** "involves a more thorough investigation. Here we are digging deeper and asking questions to gain more accurate and comprehensive information [about the people in our community. We are seeking to understand the needs of the people in our communities as well as the causes of those needs.] Engagement is the process of investigation through uncovering historical data. . . . The real needs are found in causes, not symptoms."[16] For example, if you discover there is a lot of poverty in your community, you need to uncover what's driving that poverty if you want your church to minister to that need.

A really simple way you can start the engagement process is by interviewing people in your community. When the leaders and the congregation all go out and connect with others, it causes God's people to develop a heart for the city and the gospel to work in it.

The third step is **recording.** This type of recording is similar to the descriptive work done in ethnographic recording. "An ethnographic record consists of fieldnotes, tape recordings, pictures, artifacts, and anything else that documents the social situation under study."[17] "The recording in this case pulls together descriptive information of events, causes and responses, dialogue, interview text, anything that will, in the mind of the recorder, be helpful for shedding light on the subject at hand."[18]

From this point, the church categorizes the findings and then assesses them to uncover which needs it is best poised to meet effectively. We must recognize that no church can do everything, but every church can do something.

> Because our churches have often been more focused on building buildings and creating programs than about advancing the kingdom by leveraging the talents and gifts of those within it, many have come to view the church as a task to be done rather than a community to be in. Yet, as we have seen, the church was established as the mechanism for spreading the gospel and impacting the world for good. It is to be a community of believers whose impact on the culture is greater as a whole than it ever would be individually.[19]

God's church must gather and scatter. She must be able to connect as a community to engage the city but also disperse into the various venues and spaces of influence and connection to help people meet Jesus. Consider Paul's encouragement to the church at Colossae:

> At the same time, pray also for us that God may open a door to
> us for the word, to speak the mystery of Christ, for which I am
> in chains, so that I may make it known as I should. Act wisely
> toward outsiders, making the most of the time. Let your speech
> always be gracious, seasoned with salt, so that you may know
> how you should answer each person. (Colossians 4:3–6)

Paul charged God's people to be engaged in evangelism and
mission. What I like most about this charge is that he is encouraging God's people to collectively take responsibility for being witnesses for God. "Paul urges the Colossian believers to exercise
God-given wisdom in their interactions with people they encounter at the marketplace, at work, and at civic functions."[20] "A
discussion 'seasoned with salt' became a way of referring to an
interesting, stimulating, and enjoyable conversation or discourse.
One ancient writer bemoaned the presentations of certain phi-
losophers as 'unsalted.' "[21] "Whenever the Colossian Christians
have opportunity to interact with unbelievers, Paul wants them to
engage in lively and interesting conversation. The image that he
provides of the Colossian church is not of a group who have dis-
engaged from the world and are huddling together in isolation.
His comments presuppose a group of people involved in the
community and bearing a vibrant testimony."[22]

Darrell Guder expresses this beautifully in his book, *Missional
Church*:

> It was never the responsibility of a special unit of believers to
> bear the load of reaching and engaging the lost. It is our sacred
> task to be faithful gospel witnesses in the world. We see clearly
> that Jesus's last instruction to His disciples was to make disci-
> ples, which requires being witnesses. Consequently, that is why
> the Spirit was sent. God's mission continued then in the sending

of the Spirit to call forth and empower the church as the witness to God's good news in Jesus Christ. It continues today in the worldwide witness of churches in every culture to the gospel of Jesus Christ, and it moves toward the promised consummation of God's salvation in the eschaton ("last" or "final day").[23]

MEETING PRESSING NEEDS

At my church, Epiphany Fellowship, Paul's challenge to Titus drives our outreach and mission efforts: "Let our people learn to devote themselves to good works for pressing needs, so that they will not be unfruitful" (Titus 3:14). One of the key words in this beautiful verse is *learn*. Ideally, this verse single-handedly encourages every church and believer to remain in a constant state of learning. Just as it is said about business, fixing people's problems is fundamental to connection and engagement in the church.

Over the years, our approach to outreach has greatly evolved. In the early years, we had a Christian Holy Hip-Hop and Dance outreach event. We even had mobile outreach events where we took art to the streets, and when a crowd gathered, we shared the gospel. It was a very sweet period. As time went on, we learned how complex the context in which we were ministering was. The book *101 Ways to Reach Your Community* gives categories that aided us in formulating our ministry outreach practically: It suggests conducting "blitzes," events connecting to the community, and city investments.[24] All of these are simple ways we connected with people or got their attention to introduce them to the gospel.

Blitzes

Blitzes are fun engagements that get people's feet wet in serving and loving non-Christians and are quick opportunities to make our presence known in the community.

Blitzing projects are great for the following:

- getting your people involved with an *action* orientation
- doing something that doesn't take a long *time* to pull off
- creating quick *momentum* . . .
- building initial evangelism *confidence* . . .
- expanding *vision* . . .
- seeing the *potential* for reaching out to the entire city with outreach projects[25]

Most times at these sorts of events, contact is quick, with the hope being that you've at least introduced someone to your church. God's people, for the most part, haven't been in contact with lost people in this way. Non-Christians may not readily admit it, but they most respect when the church shows care, particularly when there are no strings attached, and the saints endure in the city and don't allow this to be their only contact. As time goes on, when you consistently do blitzes and other events that serve the community, the city and neighborhood look forward to them and expect them.

On a personal note, I've seen local believers develop similar organizations that did this. One group was made up of some believers in Philly who did something called Project 215. They did work with the homeless, construction for the poor, block cleanups, clothing drives, and open-air gospel presentations. And you don't need to be a pastor to plan a blitz. There are so many practical ways that the average believer can mobilize and do blitzing opportunities.

Connecting
Connecting events help the community to experience a longer touch from the church. Our largest connecting event is called

the Diamond Street Festival. We fry hundreds of pounds of fish, give away bottles of cold water, cook mounds of BBQ, provide free haircuts, offer salon services for women, provide health screenings, and offer crisis-pregnancy support. We host a job fair, offer job training, and give away free clothing. We also have face painting, inflatable slides, and bounce houses for the kids, and we additionally offer free health classes for area residents and vending opportunities for local businesses. In a day, we see almost three thousand people. We have a prayer booth, live music, and local leaders giving talks to the community as well as gospel presentations. There are entire families in attendance, grandparents bringing their grands, and both single moms and pops bringing their kids out. It's always amazing to see. Our neighborhood and city love it. I watch our people smiling as they serve the people of our community, and it brings so much joy to my heart.

Connecting projects are great for the following:

- providing a safe place for experimenting with outreach
- a chance to truly serve the public . . .
- an opportunity to get into significant and evangelistic conversations with those being served
- a great place for families with young children to get involved with outreach ministry
- a chance to develop humble hearts[26]

Our first church plant from Epiphany Fellowship Philly, led by Dr. Doug Logan, was Epiphany Fellowship Camden. Dr. Logan had one of the most unique outreaches I've ever heard of: dog breeding. He and his crew bred American bulldogs. It was a breed that many African Americans and Latinos in Camden, New Jersey, were into. It became a life-on-life mission opportunity that led to many conversions and disciples and an amazing witness.

> Having been breeding dogs for eighteen years, I immediately saw a ministry opportunity. I encouraged others on my pastoral team to get involved, and we started our own breeding under the name "Nu City Bullies." (The name itself was an attempt to communicate gospel truth in the language of the block.) . . .
>
> Our common interest in dog breeding has provided a starting point of discussion with people who would not ordinarily want to associate with a church pastoral team. One such person was a young man named Kevin. Kevin, as we came to find out, had been a major drug dealer in the city, but he had recently begun breeding bullies. We quickly formed a bond with him through our dogs. Slowly, we were able to discuss spiritual matters and convinced him to come to church. He came to meet Jesus two years later, and I am proud to say that he has turned his life around. His story has become a powerful witness to the gospel and its transformative truth.[27]

It's stories like these that bring the gospel to life. They illustrate simple ways we can both demonstrate and proclaim the good news about Jesus. I believe that churches need to experiment with outreach. I would encourage you to try different low-cost outreaches that connect you with the people you are trying to reach. Your goal in experimenting is to develop contextual clarity on what works and what doesn't. Sometimes people will give insight into what is helpful, but many times the Holy Spirit will give us clarity through communal observations that aid in finding connection points, and those points can lead to gospel opportunities. No matter what type of context we are in, there is always something we can do to open doors for the gospel.

City Investment

Early on, we were an inner-city church, and financially we still relied on outside support, so we were unable to do any long-term projects. Therefore, it took a bit of time for our church to get to the point of city investment. City investment involves meeting a long-term need with opportunities for deeper impact. We could even call it institution building. Institutional development goes beyond events and delves into what can help rebrand a church in the community on a very deep level.

Investing projects are great for the following:

- community building
- a chance to listen deeply to the people of your city
- the greatest chance to invite people to your small group
- an opportunity to practice praying for people
- building bridges of credibility between you and the community[28]

Our church's first city-investing project was our basketball league. Many of the schools in our area didn't have well-funded or safe sports programs. At the time, Curtis Dunlap was our student ministries pastor. He took my vision for sports ministry and ran with it. We had more than 150 participants at that time, and the games were fun to watch. We passed out flyers, and kids came from all over North Philly. Teachers, staff, and even one of the principals from a local school called William D. Kelley attended a game. Families came to the games. Because we have a small relationship with the Philadelphia 76ers, we were able to play the championship game at the Wells Fargo Center in South Philly, where the 76ers play their home games. It was epic. To see families and friends enjoy themselves and young people earn trophies is indescribable. We were also able to engage many Muslim families, and soon half of our youth ministry was from Muslim families. These families knew we'd be talking about Jesus, but they viewed our ministry as a safe place and were willing to let their kids attend.

One of the things I've learned about rebranding is that we might not always see conversions or the fruits of our labor. However, the key will be that the things we do help to rebuild the image of Christ through the church in the world. As that happens, the resistance toward the church begins to dissipate. People of peace will be open to more opportunities to serve and help the city, and they can be helpful in bringing people from darkness to light. Our rebranding mission is merely to remove unnecessary obstacles to the gospel and show the love of Jesus Christ.

One of my dreams is to see believers do some online ministry on their own—through podcasts, reels, Twitch, and YouTube—that addresses many issues in culture from a Christian worldview. That is happening in some measure but could use more engagement. With the number of voices going viral in today's world, it would be great to see more Christ-centered voices among them. Since we are the redeemed of the Lord, we should be the best versions of humanity on the planet. Because of Christ's work in us, the world needs to see His work through us on all fronts.

I believe that the work of rebranding evangelism and mission falls squarely on the shoulders of every follower of Jesus. I also believe every follower of Jesus has unique contexts, giftings, and skills to bring to the table. What is your dream when it comes to evangelism and the mission God has given us? Do you even have a dream? Perhaps now is the time to develop one. Ask God how He might use your unique talents, interests, and contexts to point people to Jesus.

9

REBRANDING CHURCH MEMBERSHIP AND COMMUNITY

DO YOU LOVE THE CHURCH?

We do something at my church that you might find a little outdated: We offer what we call "the right hand of fellowship" anytime someone commits to becoming a member of our church. It's where we formally present new members. The church and the new members celebrate this event with great joy. We post a group photo with my wife and new members on social media, and they love it. I believe we should celebrate anytime someone commits to the local church. We have found that new members enjoy being celebrated and current members enjoy celebrating new people committing to our church. It is a joy and a privilege. Many people invite their family and friends, and we have a formal reception after the service. It's a sweet time. One of my favorite parts of this process is hearing people's stories about their transformation and their desire to lock in with God and His people. I've been brought to tears many times seeing the transformative work of Jesus in these people's lives.

Over the years, I've had many people (I'd estimate about four thousand) come through our church. Everyone was in different places in their lives and walks with the Lord. We've had all types: attendees, visitors, committed members, and uncommitted members. Like many growing churches, we have always had more attendees and visitors than committed members. (We haven't cracked the code on that yet.) In our new-members classes, I ask people, "What's your name? Where are you from? Why do you want to be part of Epiphany Fellowship?" I'm always amazed when people speak about how long they have been visiting. Some people say two months, but many times it has been two years or more. Recently, someone said ten years! I was thrown off. With our church, people tend to court us for a good while. It seems as though folks want to know whether our church is a legit spot to connect to, and that takes time.

We've had a few folks come to our church from a denomination that will go unnamed. I have tons of respect for the pastors I personally know in that fellowship. Some of these folks joined our church, and others kept coming in and out. It seems that some of them wanted the benefits of membership without the practical commitment of being fully invested and engaged. When I asked why they kept moving around, they simply stated that they believed in the body of Christ and felt they could just move from church to church as they "felt led," be there for a season, and then go elsewhere. At times, they caused some challenges in the ministry because it was difficult to hold them accountable and pastor them; they had a sort of free-spirited disposition about church and spiritual authority. When I questioned their approach and challenged them to commit to our church, many left for good.

CONSUMERISM VERSUS COMMUNITY

One of the challenges I've faced when teaching on church membership is helping people see that membership is not about having your personal needs met. Church membership is about investing in the body of the church. This investment does have a profound personal benefit, though: Investing in the lives of others is personally life-changing. We need to be part of the body that God created, not the one we want to have. Meeting the needs of the people who attend our churches is important, but it isn't the goal of the church. The goal of the church is to help people grow to be more like Jesus. Being a conduit for God in the lives of others is simply lit.

IS CHURCH MEMBERSHIP BIBLICAL?

There is no prescribed membership process in the New Testament per se; however, there are descriptive passages in the Bible that demonstrate that the early church was clear on who was part of the church and who wasn't. From Genesis on, the Most High was always concerned about who were His people and who were not, and He counted them. Genesis 46:27 says, "Joseph's sons who were born to him in Egypt: two persons. All those of Jacob's household who came to Egypt: seventy persons." In Numbers 1:17–46, we find the census of God's people after escaping slavery in Egypt. We learn that there were 603,550 men aged twenty and up. It is estimated that the number of those in Israel was well over two million. In other words, God has always been invested in counting and identifying His people.

Acts 2:41 tells us that three thousand people converted to Christ when Peter preached at Pentecost. We can draw a number of important lessons for the church from this information. Peter and the apostles kept count of converts. They also devised a system of recognizing who was part of the faith community and who wasn't. This shouldn't surprise us given that the Lord keeps track of those who are His (Revelation 13:8). Therefore, church members are

> Christians who actively participate in the life of the local church so that it is built up for God's purposes for the kingdom locally, nationally, and internationally (1 Corinthians 12). The early church's notion of covenant community membership included numerical records (Acts 2:37–47), records of widows (1 Timothy 5:3–16), elections (Acts 6:1–6), discipline (Matthew 18:15–20; 1 Corinthians 5; Galatians 6:1), accountability (Hebrews 13:17), and an awareness of who was a church covenant community member (Romans 16:1–16).[1]

Church membership isn't optional; it's an essential part of the process God uses to grow us into the image of Jesus. You need the support, accountability, and care of a committed body of believers, and that same body of believers needs you.

PRACTICAL REASONS FOR CHURCH MEMBERSHIP

All believers are, in a sense, part of the body of Christ. That is, of course, a theological reality, but it doesn't change the fact that the Bible calls us to commit to a local body of believers. We have to ask ourselves this: What does practical connection to the people of God look like on a local level? I'd say not having a clear membership process and keeping records of members could be irresponsible. Knowing clearly who has put their hands to the plow in a particular vineyard is important.

CLARITY OF EXPECTATIONS

The Bible commands pastors to shepherd the flock (see 1 Peter 5:1–4). Just because people attend doesn't mean they have officially come under the authority of the Word or the guidance, protection, and leadership of a church's local leaders. Leaders need clarity, and so do those who are part of a local flock. If we reject the idea of church membership, then all pastors are everyone's pastors and all flocks are everyone's flocks. Most churches that I know of have more attendees than committed members, and, frankly, that scares me. Today, we need order more than ever. That doesn't mean believers should isolate themselves from anyone outside their local church, as that is cultlike behavior. I do think, however, that believers should devote themselves to loving, caring for, and serving the people in their local church. There are close to sixty "one another" commands in the New Testament. The commands are written to believers living in community with local churches and remind us that we, as leaders, have a spiritual responsibility to the people in our local church and they have a spiritual responsibility to us. These commands—such as "Love one another" (John 13:34), "Pray for one another" (James 5:16), and "Carry one another's burdens" (Galatians 6:2)—paint a clear picture of how God expects believers to live in community: close enough to see one another struggle and close enough to help. The "one another" commands, which will be explored later, form the practical connective tissue of true gospel community.

I believe establishing clarity around how membership works in your church is one of the most caring and responsible things a church can do. During the Covid-19 pandemic, I assigned our leaders to call every single covenant community member in the church and check on their well-being and needs. Those who responded were delighted. However, we chose not to call those who merely attended but were not members. In many ways, we aren't spiritually responsible for their souls on the same level as those who are members. They are not functionally connected to us in a way that gives us jurisdiction to lovingly care for them. Paul's home church was the church at Antioch (see Acts 13). He was sent there by the leadership and came back later to report on his ministry efforts abroad (see 15:22). The only reason he reported to the Jerusalem church was because the church in Jerusalem was the central authority at that time due to the apostles who were there.

Here's how Jonathan Leeman defines church membership in his book *The Church and the Surprising Offense of God's Love*:

> Church membership is (1) a covenant of union between a particular church and a Christian, a covenant that consists of (2) the church's affirmation of the Christian's gospel profession, (3) the church's promise to give oversight to the Christian, and (4) the Christian's promise to gather with the church and submit to its oversight.[2]

And as Bobby Jamieson says,

1. Church membership is a covenant. That is, it's a solemn agreement between a Christian and a local church. In this covenant:
2. The church affirms the Christian's profession of faith in Christ. That is, by extending church membership to an individual, the church is saying, "As far as we can tell, you're a Christian. We're putting our seal of approval on your claim to follow Christ."
3. The church promises to oversee the Christian's discipleship. This comes through teaching, preaching, the elders' oversight, and the mutual building up, which all members of the church are to engage in (see Eph. 4:11–16).

4. The Christian promises to regularly assemble with and submit to the church. By committing to a church through membership, an individual Christian promises to regularly gather with this church and to submit to its authority and teaching.[3]

So, at my church, before we accept anyone into membership, we ask that they take a four-session new-members course. If you've never been part of a church that does something like this, it might seem extreme, but the goal is simply to help people who want to join our church understand what they are getting themselves into. There is so much misinformation out there about what the church is and what it does that we feel it's important to bring clarity to those who want to join us. Here is a quick outline of what that four-session course looks like:

Session 1—The Gospel. We discuss creation, sin, and salvation. The goal in this session is to make sure anyone who wants to join our church not only understands the gospel but also believes it. We want to confirm that those who join our church have truly trusted Christ.

Session 2—The Church. Here we discuss what a healthy church looks like. We also discuss the sacraments and evangelism.

Session 3—Stewardship. Here we discuss every member's responsibility and calling to invest their time, money, and energy into the church. We discuss how members are called to use their spiritual gifts to glorify God and build up the church.

Session 4—Core Values. Here we discuss the particulars of our church: our mission and values and also core beliefs. This ses-

sion helps people understand who we are and what we are trying to do by God's grace. In this session, we also discuss our
church's membership covenant and leadership covenant.

A membership covenant is a set of agreements that every
member of the church agrees to live by. It involves a commitment
to meet regularly, love and serve one another, and hold one another accountable as we each seek to follow Jesus in our daily
lives. We also have a leadership covenant. This is a set of promises
that the leaders of our church make to the members of the
church. It includes promises such as these:

- We commit ourselves to lovingly caring for you and
  seeking your growth in Christ (1 Thessalonians 5:12;
  Hebrews 13:17).
- We covenant to provide teaching and counsel from
  Scripture (Galatians 6:6; 1 Timothy 5:17–18).
- We commit that this teaching will span the whole
  counsel of God's Word (Acts 20:27–28).
- We commit to helping you in times of need (Acts 2:
  42–47; 4:32–35; James 2:14–17).
- We pledge to help you become equipped to serve
  Christ (Ephesians 4:11–13).
- We covenant to seek God's will for our church
  community to the best of our ability as we study Scripture
  and follow the Spirit (Acts 20:28; 1 Peter 5:1–5).
- We pledge to set an example and join you in fulfilling the
  duties of covenant community members (1 Corinthians
  11:1; Philippians 3:17; 1 Timothy 4:12).

The goal of this covenant is to let our members know that the
pastors and leaders of our church are committed to loving, serving, and leading them faithfully. It rightly reflects the higher call-

ing expected of leaders as they seek to set an example for the church.

COVENANT COMMUNITY EXPECTATIONS

Here is what we ask people who want to join our church to commit to doing:

- Embrace the vision, values, and strategy.
- Participate in public and private gatherings.
- Pray for the ministry and one another regularly.
- Serve faithfully in some capacity.
- Give financially to Epiphany Fellowship.
- Gather others, both believers and unbelievers, to Epiphany through evangelism and discipleship.

We have our candidates write out their conversion stories. Following that, our deacons interview each candidate to gauge whether the candidates are believers based on their ability to articulate the gospel through both their stories and live engagement.

Then, on a designated Sunday, we give "the right hand of fellowship" (Galatians 2:9).[4] On this day, the pastors of our church shake the hands of the new members in front of the congregation to formally bring them into the local body. We shake hands because we are publicly agreeing to love and care for one another and help one another follow Jesus.

GIVING AN ACCOUNT

Hebrews 13:17 says, "Obey your leaders and submit to them, for they keep watch over your souls and will give an account for their work. Let them do this with joy and not with complaints, for this would be no advantage for you" (NET). I am not sure many church leaders take this passage seriously, especially the part about giving an account. How can you give an account for those who have not been carefully accounted for? I believe we as leaders will be judged for how we shepherd the flock, including how our people follow biblical and healthy leadership in the local church of which they are a part:

> Hebrews recognizes that the whole community is summoned to be watchful against sin and bitterness and to care for others through encouragement and exhortation (note 3:12–13; 12:15). But leaders have a special, God-given responsibility to do this. . . . Godly leaders are diligent and tireless. They look after the lives of all in their care, but particularly those who are negligent or prone to spiritual laziness, or who fail to recognize the importance of fellowship with other believers (2:3; 5:11; 6:12; 10:25).[5]

Revelation 2:5 makes it clear that there is an official lampstand in heaven that represents every official local church on earth. This further affirms that local church connection matters to God. Biblical submission to the church and its leadership should be a deep part of our DNA. For instance, when I wanted to plant a church, I wanted to have clear affirmation from a sending church because I believe God uses local leaders and the people in the congregation to affirm our calling. I know I want the leaders who have mentored me over the years to give me rave reviews at the judgment seat of Christ.

GETTING BACK TO THE IDEA OF BIBLICAL COMMUNITY

When God saved us, He reconciled us not only to Himself but also to one another. We are saved to be in relationship with Him and in relationship with His people. The Bible says, "He has rec-onciled you by his physical body through his death, to present you holy, faultless, and blameless before him" (Colossians 1:22). "For we were all baptized by one Spirit into one body—whether Jews or Greeks, whether slaves or free—and we were all given one Spirit to drink" (1 Corinthians 12:13). "Christ died for his people, and we are saved when, by faith, we become part of the people for whom Christ died."[6] This is not to say that church membership saves us. God saves us, but He saves us into commu-nity. "The story of the Bible is the story of God's fulfilling the promise, 'I will take you as my own people, and I will be your God' (Exodus 6:7; Revelation 21:3). If the gospel is to be at the heart of church life and mission, it is equally true that the church is to be at the heart of gospel life and mission."[7]

Paul says that we are "members of one another" (Romans 12:5). We as believers must own that in the realest way possible. Most people make their decision to commit to Jesus in connec-tion with people. One of the things I value about the new genera-tion is that they take relationships seriously. That quality just needs Jesus at the center of it. Community is the way that church shows itself to be a family.

Acts 2:42–47 demonstrates how the early church deeply val-ued community. They were involved in each other's lives and held close personal relationships with one another. Verse 42 implies that the people of the early church saw caring, devoted commu-nity as a fundamental value of being a disciple of Jesus Christ. It didn't seem to be an option but rather was part of being saved— the redemption of their relationship with God and one another. Not only are we restored in our relationship to God, but we are restored and reconciled to one another. The early church's fellow-ship wasn't forced; it was a delight and was embraced with great enthusiasm.

One of the most beautiful parts of community in the New Testament is that it crossed socioeconomic lines. Although the community was messy at times, the people still were willing to engage in it. Establishing community in the early church also resulted in many cultural challenges, as Paul details in Galatians 2 and Luke demonstrates in Acts 6. We can't allow our fear of being hurt to affect our view of community. The gospel assumes the presence of hurt and the need for forgiveness and restoration.

Community is one of the foremost core values of the New Testament. More than merely an organization, the church is a living organism. That should radically change how we think about and approach our relationship with our local churches. Christians must develop a robust understanding of community and its role in our sanctification and growth.

It is important to remember that Paul's churches were made up of both Jews and Gentiles, two groups of people who seemingly had very little in common and harbored a tremendous amount of distrust against one another, yet Paul encouraged them to "work . . . especially for those of the family of faith" (Galatians 6:10, NRSV). In Paul's mind, trusting Jesus should radically reshape how these disparate people think about themselves and about one another. Through Christ, "both have access in one Spirit to the Father" and "are fellow citizens with the saints and members of the household of God" (Ephesians 2:18–19, ESV).

One of the most important things a church must do is build spaces for people to relationally engage. Whether it's small groups, outings, retreats, or game nights, churches should provide means of connection. For the "one another" commands to be practiced, we must be in the presence of one another. No matter the means, we as the people of God must facilitate this.

One time, a person was considering leaving my church. They communicated that they were having a problem connecting. I asked them what service they went to, what small group they were part of, and where they were serving. They began to tell me they only came on Sunday. It seemed they valued being engaged, but they wanted people to come to them.

Fundamentally, the "one another" commands signal mutual communal commitment. Real Christian faith walks are built on people's taking the initiative to follow Christ. The local church is all hands on deck. There are times when someone is hurting, sick, wayward, or dealing with some struggle and needs to be engaged and sought after. Emergencies and chronic needs shouldn't be the only reasons that people are sought after. We should build such a thoughtful relational culture that being connected to one another comes naturally. Other than that, all believers need to engage and view themselves as disciples on a mission, not consumers in a store.

Take a moment and read through the following list of the "one another" commands. What do the verses tell you about how you should participate in the local church?

"Be at peace with one another." (Mark 9:50)

"Wash one another's feet." (John 13:14)

"Love one another." (John 13:34)

"Have love for one another." (John 13:35, NKJV)

"Love one another." (John 15:12)

"Love one another." (John 15:17)

"Be devoted to one another in brotherly love." (Romans 12:10, NASB)

"Honor one another above yourselves." (Romans 12:10, NIV)

"Live in harmony with one another." (Romans 12:16, ESV)

"Love one another." (Romans 13:8)

"Stop passing judgment on one another." (Romans 14:13, NIV)

"Accept one another, just as Christ also accepted us." (Romans 15:7, NASB)

"Instruct one another." (Romans 15:14)

"Greet one another with a holy kiss." (Romans 16:16)

"When you come together to eat, wait for one another." (1 Corinthians 11:33, NKJV)

"Have equal concern for each other." (1 Corinthians 12:25, NIV)

"Greet one another with a holy kiss." (1 Corinthians 16:20)

"Greet one another with a holy kiss." (2 Corinthians 13:12)

"Serve one another through love." (Galatians 5:13)

"If you bite and devour one another, . . . you will be consumed by one another." (Galatians 5:15)

"Let us not become conceited, provoking one another, envying one another." (Galatians 5:26)

"Bear one another's burdens." (Galatians 6:2, NKJV)

"Be patient, bearing with one another in love." (Ephesians 4:2, NIV)

"Be kind and compassionate to one another." (Ephesians 4:32)

"Forgiv[e] one another." (Ephesians 4:32)

"[Speak] to one another in psalms, hymns, and spiritual songs." (Ephesians 5:19)

"[Submit] to one another out of reverence for Christ." (Ephesians 5:21, ESV)

"In humility regard others as better than yourselves." (Philippians 2:3, NRSV)

"Do not lie to one another." (Colossians 3:9)

"Bear with one another." (Colossians 3:13, NRSV)

"Forgiving one another if anyone has a grievance against another." (Colossians 3:13)

"Teach . . . one another." (Colossians 3:16, NRSV)

"Admonish one another." (Colossians 3:16, NRSV)

"Increase and overflow with love for one another." (1 Thessalonians 3:12)

"Love one another." (1 Thessalonians 4:9)

"Comfort one another." (1 Thessalonians 4:18, NKJV)

"Comfort each other." (1 Thessalonians 5:11, NKJV)

"Edify one another." (1 Thessalonians 5:11, NKJV)

"Encourage one another day after day." (Hebrews 3:13, NASB)

"Spur one another on toward love and good deeds." (Hebrews 10:24, NIV)

"Encourage one another." (Hebrews 10:25, NLT)

"Do not slander one another." (James 4:11, NIV)

"Do not grumble against one another." (James 5:9, NKJV)

"Confess your sins to one another." (James 5:16)

"Pray for one another." (James 5:16)

"Hav[e] compassion for one another." (1 Peter 3:8, NKJV)

"Be harmonious." (1 Peter 3:8, NASB)

"Have fervent love for one another." (1 Peter 4:8, NKJV)

"Be hospitable to one another without grumbling." (1 Peter 4:9, NKJV)

"Each of you should use whatever gift you have received to serve others." (1 Peter 4:10, NIV)

"Clothe yourselves with humility toward one another." (1 Peter 5:5)

"Greet one another with a kiss of love." (1 Peter 5:14)

"Love one another." (1 John 3:11)

"Love one another." (1 John 3:23)

"Love one another." (1 John 4:7)
"Love one another." (1 John 4:11)
"Love one another." (1 John 4:12)
"Love one another." (2 John 5)

After reading this list, how do you sense the Holy Spirit guiding you to strengthen your relationships? How might you invest more deeply in the members of your church?

Healthy community is organized and intentional. In essence, the church has a responsibility to do and make space for certain things, but every believer also has their own responsibility to build relationships and make space for community. My greatest prayer in this season is for a revival of local church commitment. I believe it is happening on some levels. One thing we must all work on is being an attractional safe place for people to lock into the mission of God's kingdom on earth.

10

REBRANDING JESUS CHRIST

ZEITGEIST IS A DOCUMENTARY THAT CAME OUT A WHILE AGO.[1] THERE was also a book released called *The Jesus Mysteries*.[2] I surveyed the book and watched some clips from the documentary, and both seemed to rehash accounts of the old eighteenth-century mystics who said that Jesus was a myth and the stories about Him copied Egyptian allegories. As the internet grew, so did the urban legends. False ideologies about Christianity and the person of Jesus Christ spread that denied Jesus as the Messiah from many angles. This included some ideologies that we have already discussed, such as the Black Conscious Community, Black Hebrew Israelites, Hebrew roots movement, and deconstruction movement, but among them are also witchcraft, African spirituality, and atheism. Each of these groups has a false or deficient view of Jesus. Some see Him as merely an example; others see Him as a metaphor, impostor, prophet, real person blown out of proportion, or, in some instances, pure fiction.

There are even groups within the church that have heterodox, or heretical, views of Jesus. Some say He was a created being or that He had to *earn* His God status. Some are modalistic, meaning they believe that Jesus wasn't a distinct person but rather a manifestation of God. Recently, many Christians have realized that Seventh-day Adventists (SDA) hold to this heretical doctrine and can be considered a cult.

Adventists believe in a great conflict between God and Satan that they visualize as an arm-wrestling match, centered around the Ten Commandments, in which God and Satan vie for supremacy. According to Adventists, the conflict started when God promoted Jesus to deity status. Satan, jealous of Jesus, thought he was better suited for that promotion. The SDA pre-creation narrative, formulated by author Ellen G. White's dreams and visions, taught that Jesus was not always God but was originally Michael the Archangel.

In that narrative, God eventually "invited" Jesus into His counsel and exalted Him to be equal to Himself. Satan, angered by Jesus's promotion, campaigned against God and His law throughout heaven and the "unfallen worlds." Some angels were convinced by Satan's arguments and joined him. As a result, according to this outlook, God is now embroiled in a dispute with Satan, aiming to vindicate His character, prove that His law is just and can be kept, disprove Satan's accusations, and win the eternal loyalty of His subjects.

WHAT IS CHRISTOLOGY?

Christology is the study and understanding of the Bible's revelation of the person and work of Jesus Christ. Lately, I have been on a tirade of sorts—I'd say a holy and righteous one—the reason being that many believers aren't very discerning today. They lack the basic biblical acumen to know which messages about Jesus are true and authentic and which are not. Sadly, the church has done a poor job of teaching people who Jesus is.

When introducing people to Jesus, we must clearly teach about the following:

His preexistence: Unlike everything else in creation, Jesus was not created but existed eternally with the Father.

His incarnation: Jesus, while fully God, chose to take on human flesh and dwell among us.

His exaltation: When Jesus rose from the dead, God proved His authority over sin and death and established Jesus as the King of a new, eternal kingdom.

Fundamentally, Christology is about who Jesus is and what He has done. Understanding who Jesus—His person—is must be everything to the believer: "This is eternal life: that they may know you, the only true God, and the one you have sent—Jesus Christ" (John 17:3). Knowing Jesus is both relational and cognitive. It's not merely intellectual, but relationship building requires knowledge about the person you are building with: "Eternal life turns on nothing more and nothing less than knowledge of the true God. Eternal life is not so much everlasting life as personal knowledge of the Everlasting One."[3]

WHO IS JESUS?

Jesus asked this question of His disciples, realizing that He was an important part of His ministry. He constantly stated that if you don't recognize Him, you don't recognize the Father (see John 14:8–14). Jesus constantly chastised the religious leadership of His day for not connecting the dots in the Old Testament and thus failing to recognize who He was and why He came. He asserted to John the Baptist that His ministry fulfilled Isaiah 61:1–2, challenged Nicodemus to understand the concept from Scripture of being born again (see Ezekiel 36:25–28; John 3), and, on the road to Emmaus, gave a Christological tour through the law, prophets, and writings (see Luke 24:13–27).

Jesus's nature is one of the most beautiful doctrines in the Bible. He is 100 percent God and 100 percent human—two natures unmixed in one person forever. Theologians call that the hypostatic union. Paul says that Jesus, "existing in the form of God, did not consider equality with God as something to be exploited. Instead he emptied himself by assuming the form of a servant, taking on the likeness of humanity" (Philippians 2:6–7). Paul uses the word form twice: once to describe Jesus's relation to God and once to describe His relationship to humankind. Form in the Greek is the word morphē, which means essence, nature, character, or "the expression of something (such as a visual, spatial, or preternatural expression) that reflects or manifests fully and truly (and permanently) the essence of what something is."[4] As it pertains to humanity, Jesus shares the qualities in His body, soul, and spirit of what makes man "man." In the same way, He is, in His deity, what the Father and Spirit are: co-equal and co-eternal in attributes and perfection. He is without sin! He is everything that makes God "God," with full holiness and perfection.

The phrase "existing in the form of God" (verse 6) is profound. It means that during His time on earth, Jesus did not stop being God. However, He "emptied himself," meaning He laid aside the independent use of His eternal attributes during His earthly ministry. Both of His natures are necessary for redemption. As a man, Christ could represent humanity and die as a man; as God, Christ's death could have infinite value "sufficient to provide redemption for the sins of the world."[5]

Understanding this prevents us from reducing Jesus to our

favorite parts or editing out what doesn't fit our desired traits. God doesn't have system settings; you can't adjust Him to fit your desires and standards. He comes factory ready with no ability to be changed. This understanding lets us know we don't have an evolving God. The Bible says that Jesus "is the same yesterday, today, and forever" (Hebrews 13:8).

Philippians 2:7 talks about Jesus emptying Himself. Some people say He emptied His deity and was no longer God in His humanity, but that couldn't be further from the truth. Jesus was still fully God but took on an additional nature. The beauty of Jesus's coming to earth was His restraint: "Christ merely surrendered the independent exercise of some of his relative or transitive attributes. He did not surrender the absolute or immanent attributes in any sense; He was always perfectly holy, just, merciful, truthful, and faithful."[6] The context of verse 7 provides the best solution to the kenosis problem. "The term *kenosis* comes from the Greek word for the doctrine of Christ's self-emptying in His incarnation. The kenosis was a self-renunciation, not an emptying Himself of deity nor an exchange of deity for humanity. Philippians 2:7 tells us that Jesus 'emptied Himself, taking the form of a bond-servant, and being made in the likeness of men.' Jesus did not cease to be God during His earthly ministry. But He did set aside His heavenly glory of a face-to-face relationship with God. He also set aside His independent authority."[7] The emptying was not a subtraction but rather an *addition*. The following four phrases (see verses 7–8) explain the emptying: "(a) taking the form of a bond-servant, and (b) being made in the likeness of men. And (c) being found in appearance as a man, (d) He humbled Himself by becoming obedient to the point of death. The 'emptying' of Christ meant taking on an additional nature: a human nature with its limitations. His deity was never surrendered."[8]

In John 12, John quotes Isaiah 6 and applies it to Jesus, indicating that Jesus is YHWH, the one seated on the high throne talking to Isaiah. John Oswalt points out that this passage "shows Jesus as ruler over all things and demonstrates that God's presence is not restricted to a temple but fills the whole earth."[9]

Submitting to Jesus as Lord begins with understanding His essential nature: fully God and fully human. The more you embrace Jesus truly, the more your heart will long to submit to Him and the more you'll find yourself actively living like He does.

A soldier was frustrated with his drill sergeant because of how much the sergeant was demanding of them. This soldier wasn't the only one who felt that way. Consequently, the drill instructor said, "I'm not telling you to do anything I haven't done or am not willing to do!" The instructor then put on a fifty-pound backpack and began running to show that it was possible. From there, he ran the entire ten miles with them while carrying the same amount of weight they were carrying. The soldiers felt better and even respected the sergeant more because of it. Likewise, Jesus Christ has gone before us and is going with us.

WHAT DID JESUS COME TO DO?

There are many conflicting views today about Jesus's mission. Even in His day, people had various expectations of a messiah. John 1:18 provides the thesis and purpose statement of Jesus's ministry: "No one has ever seen God. The one and only Son, who is himself God and is at the Father's side—he has revealed him." Jesus came to reveal the Father to the world, which does not know the Father or what He is like. The Greek word for *reveal* means "to make fully and clearly known."[10] What qualified Jesus to do that? He has seen the Father, is Himself God, and is at the Father's side. Although Moses was told by God that no human can see Him and live (see Exodus 33:20), Jesus, both before coming to earth and after His ascension, can be face-to-face with God and dwell in the same "unapproachable light" (1 Timothy 6:16) as the Father in the most holy place in heaven.

Jesus makes plain for us who God is. He is "the way, the truth, and the life" (John 14:6). Telling people that Jesus is the only way to God is not judgmental or offensive; it's one of the most loving things you can say because no one else can lead the way to God.

Right now, there is a sector of the black church that is becoming extremely heretical. The group's understanding of the infallibility and inerrancy of Scripture, the personhood of God, the gospel, and the exclusivity of Jesus is up for grabs. In a sector of the charismatic world, there are also some strange beliefs beginning to take hold about who Jesus is and what He came to do. Teachers in those movements claim that Jesus came to help us be little gods.

In addition, people who have been raised in the church are becoming comfortable with witchcraft. Witchcraft is the attempt to get illegitimate access to the spirit realm. Deuteronomy explicitly tells us that God is opposed to it: "No one among you is to sacrifice his son or daughter in the fire, practice divination, tell fortunes, interpret omens, practice sorcery, cast spells, consult a medium or a spiritist, or inquire of the dead" (Deuteronomy 18:10–11). Those acts of idolatry will destroy a person's life, and gateways opened through witchcraft can be closed only by the power of the Holy Spirit. Our only authorized mediator between us and the spirit realm is the Lord Jesus Christ. We must brand Him as the only certified and satisfying connection to God. His supremacy is unmatched.

We must know that these rulers, principalities, and demonic goons are all under Jesus's authority. Jesus is better, as Paul makes clear in Colossians 2:8–10: "Be careful that no one takes you cap-

tive through philosophy and empty deceit based on human tradition, based on the elements of the world, rather than Christ. For
the entire fullness of God's nature dwells bodily in Christ, and
you have been filled by him, who is the head over every ruler and
authority."

Our enemy will do what he can to get us to drift away from
the faith. "Not only does the power and authority of God belong
to the resurrected Christ, but believers share in it by virtue of
their union with him. [If you trust Jesus, you] do not need to fear
the evil supernatural realm. . . . [You] have direct and immediate
access to the power of God through Christ."[11] Just like the Colossians in their day, we must know that we have a satisfactory connection to God through what Jesus has done for us: His death on
the cross and resurrection from the grave.

In that, we have a full and sufficient Savior, which gives those
of us who have trusted Jesus by faith more-than-satisfactory salvation. "Just as Jesus was fully God, believers are fully complete in
him."[12] There is nothing lacking in the salvation Jesus provides.
Our understanding of salvation may grow, and our appropriation
of the blessings of salvation may increase, but in Christ, we have
all we will ever need: the "fullness" of salvation.[13] Our understanding of Jesus deeply influences how we view our salvation. In
a very practical sense, my understanding of Him aids my soul on
every level and deepens my confidence and resolve in life.

WHAT CHRIST ARE WE PRESENTING TO THE WORLD?

In a changing culture, our understanding of who Jesus is must
never change. Many in the West view Jesus as a white European,
and for many people that image represents anything but freedom.
For many in the black community, there is a sense that Jesus was
pushed on blacks by white European slave owners to brainwash

us into being docile in our chattel enslavement. In light of this, many black people see Christianity as untrustworthy. Such "branding" is an intellectual and emotional barrier to the faith. Even outside of black circles, the far left has viewed Jesus and the Christian faith as oppressive. Many of them have attempted to rebrand Jesus in the image of societal norms. For many on the left, love is now the code word for acceptance and openness to what people feel in the existential life sphere, which is another way to describe relativism.

Relativism asserts that there are no universally valid truths or principles.[14] This worldview "clearly conflicts with the Christian gospel, which affirms there are universal truths that apply to all people in all cultures."[15] What's going on in culture does not determine truth; God does. We live in a "my truth is my truth, and your truth is yours" culture. For instance, in the whole gender dysphoria conversation, anyone can choose to be whatever gender they want, no matter their biological sex. When people do that, they call it "walking in one's truth."

Renewing something we lost requires that we stand on the truth of God's Word no matter what society says. Jesus is said to be "full of grace and truth" (John 1:14). Not only is He controlled by grace, but He is also controlled by truth. When He was praying for the cup of God's wrath to pass, if He were "walking in His truth," He would have avoided the Cross; however, he said, "Not my will, but yours, be done" (Luke 22:42).

KEY VALUES OF JESUS'S BRAND

The Christian faith has many values, such as the fruit of the Spirit, faith, hope, and love. I believe that certain points about the character of our faith need to be highlighted if we are going to represent our savior to the world. In our pluralistic and relativistic society, we must strive to value Christlike love, dying to self, and a deep affection and commitment to both the universal and local church.

Love is a powerful word that is thrown around a lot, but few people define love based on God's view of what it really is. Truth and grace are the foundations of true biblical love. Earlier, we talked about Jesus's being full of grace and truth. He moved that way constantly in His life and ministry. Love looks different based on what we need in a certain moment. To most people today, love seems to mean blind acceptance or grace without accountability. When someone does something wrong or commits an offense, it is not loving to act as though it didn't happen. Love engages wrongs head-on with hope. Love upholds justice without being unrighteously angry. Scripture teaches us to be angry but to not sin (see Ephesians 4:26–27). God disciplines those He loves, and if you aren't disciplined, you aren't His (see Hebrews 12:6).

The book of Proverbs says beautifully, "Faithful are the wounds of a friend, but deceitful are the kisses of an enemy" (27:6, NASB). Painful words from someone who loves you are called faithful. They are reliable, sure, trustworthy. God's Word reminds us that "the wounds of a friend" can be trusted because they are meant to correct and not destroy. A person who is a yes-man or someone who won't keep it real with you is deceitful.

On another front, there are those who are judgmental. Being judgmental describes someone who forms lots of opinions— usually harsh or critical ones—about lots of people. Sometimes judgmental people are right but just lack grace. Other times, people have a particular worldview about something and they're part of a tribe that is full of cognitive dissonance, keeping them from maintaining healthy judgment.

In comparison, biblical love judges rightly and isn't judgmental. The Bible teaches, "He who is spiritual appraises all things, yet he himself is appraised by no one" (1 Corinthians 2:15, NASB). So, biblical love doesn't make assumptions; it investigates, seeks the truth, and engages the truth lovingly.

Proms today are way more over-the-top than when I was growing up. In my day, we got our tux, corsage, and car or limo; the girls wore nice dresses; and we went to the prom and then to IHOP because it stayed open all night. Nowadays, proms involve full-set theme packages, red carpets, police escorts, horse-drawn carriages, a convoy of luxury cars, and hired photographers for the night. I'm all for a good time, but my kids aren't getting all that for their prom—at least not from me. I'd say I like spoiling my kids to an extent, but I want to set them up to win in life. I do what I can to help them not develop a sense of entitlement. Entitlement is an enemy of the gospel. It's the enemy of the kind of dying-to-self Jesus calls us to (see Matthew 16:24). Today, there are women who want only high-value men, which is understandable, but often what they require is unbelievable. Overall, we live in a society where entitlement has slid into narcissism. There's nothing wrong with a level of self-love and care. We are fearfully and wonderfully made. We must value ourselves because we have tremendous God-given value as His image bearers. However, in our society, self-love has been taken to destructive extremes. I think sometimes people even excuse their own selfish decisions as bids to promote their mental health.

American culture has embraced the value of self-admiration with a big, warm hug. As an NBC public service announcement puts it, "You may not realize it, but everyone is born with their one true love—themselves. If you like you, everyone else will, too." One young man expressed this view by covering his entire right side with a tattoo saying "Believe in Yourself" in graffiti-style writing (with "Rely on No One" written underneath).

Every culture is shaped by its fundamental core beliefs, and in America today there are few values more fiercely held than the importance of self-admiration. Most of us don't tattoo it on our bodies, but it is tattooed onto the flesh of our body of cultural beliefs.[16]

We should have seen it coming. "Know this: Hard times will come in the last days. For people will be lovers of self, lovers of money, boastful, proud, demeaning" (2 Timothy 3:1–2). They're concerned chiefly with oneself and one's own advantages to the exclusion of others.

In contrast, in the Scriptures, we are called to die to self. In a narcissistic, hedonistic, relativistic society, pleasure is supreme. That is the antithesis of what the Bible teaches we are to be branded by as believers. Every believer is called to bear their cross and carry their own load (see Luke 9:23; Galatians 6:5).

Remember the Dietrich Bonhoeffer quote I shared back in chapter 4? "When Christ calls a man, he bids him come and die" is one of the most famous quotes on discipleship outside the Bible.[17] Our society teaches the value of a come-up, but the Bible teaches that the way up is down—humility leads to exaltation; pride leads to humiliation. "I urge you to present your bodies as a living sacrifice, holy and pleasing to God; this is your true worship" (Romans 12:1). The terms living, holy, and pleasing show how profound the sacrifice Christ calls us to make really is. Old Testament "sacrifices were dead. As has often been quipped about this text, 'The problem with living sacrifices is that they keep crawling off the altar.' "[18]

As believers, we live every day on an altar. Why? As Paul says, "We always carry the death of Jesus in our body, so that the life of Jesus may also be displayed in our body. For we who live are always being given over to death for Jesus's sake, so that Jesus's life may also be displayed in our mortal flesh" (2 Corinthians 4: 10–11). In this era of self-promotion, purpose drivenness, new-season theology, and your-best-life-now ideology, this ancient realization from Paul needs reviving in the church of Jesus Christ.

"I love the church"—this is not something I often hear people say today. In fact, many Christians are quite cynical when talking about the church. Recently, an artist stated on a fairly large platform that "the church is wack."[19] He attempted to qualify this statement by stating that he was talking about only the institution and not every individual church, but the damage was done. I understood what the brother was saying, but the world doesn't need further fodder for feeling disappointed with the church. Disparaging it is an easy way to get an amen from the world. Ultimately, we need to rebrand how we talk about the church. We must highlight and promote what our churches are doing in their communities. We must show the people in our communities that our churches are building institutions, helping youth, starting schools, assisting with people in crisis, and speaking truth to power. Jesus says in the Sermon on the Mount,

> You are the salt of the earth. But if the salt should lose its taste, how can it be made salty? It's no longer good for anything but to be thrown out and trampled under people's feet.
>
> You are the light of the world. A city situated on a hill cannot be hidden. No one lights a lamp and puts it under a basket, but rather on a lampstand, and it gives light for all who are in the house. (Matthew 5:13–15)

In that time, salt was used for seasoning, preservation, and fertilizing soil. The point of Jesus's illustration was that the people of God would be useful and helpful in spreading His kingdom to the earth. At the end of the day, rebranding the church means earning the right to show people our glorious Savior through developing common ground with the world. God's love is so deep for the church that He sent His Son. Jesus so loves the church that He died for us. The Holy Spirit so loved the church that He keeps us for Christ's return.

In this exploration of Christology, we've delved into the true nature of Jesus, His mission, and the values that should define His followers. We've seen how crucial it is to understand and present an accurate picture of Christ in a world filled with misconceptions and relativism. Now it's your turn to take up this mantle.

As a believer, you are called to be an active participant in rebranding the church and pointing the world to Jesus. This isn't just about defending doctrine; it's about living out the transformative power of the gospel in your daily life. Challenge yourself to embody Christ's love, embrace the call to die to self, and cultivate a deep, unashamed love for the church. In your interactions, your social media presence, and your community involvement, seek opportunities to showcase the true Jesus and the positive impact of His church. Remember, you are the salt and light of the world. Your authentic representation of Christ and His body can be the catalyst that draws others to the life-changing truth of the gospel. Will you accept this challenge and join in the vital work of reintroducing the world to the real Jesus and His beloved church?

ACKNOWLEDGMENTS

I have to take the time to bless the Lord of Hosts, who stirred my soul about issues in our world and culture. I am grateful He has given me sight to see things from His perspective and hopefully call the church back to His vision and purpose for us.

To my wife, Yvette. You have encouraged me to speak what God says. You hold me accountable for how I use my voice. You constantly remind me of the mantle given to us and caution me to steward it well.

To my children! Everything I write is for you. I want my pen to draft a legacy of gospel clarity for when I'm gone, a biblical blueprint for your lives and the lives of those who come after you.

To my big sis, Lisa, for encouraging me throughout this process.

To Epiphany Fellowship. You are my letters (see 2 Corinthians 3:2–3). My post in the vineyard of God. One of the many things I love about you is that we are working out the issues highlighted in this book in real time for the glory of Jesus. Let's keep on moving. Also to Moriah, my executive assistant. You are a godsent blessing.

To those who helped complete this project. Jevon, your representation of my work is stellar, Christ glorifying, and absolutely essential. You understand what God has called me to do, and you work to communicate that at any cost. Drew and the crew at Waterbrook and Multnomah: Your confidence and investment in this work is of paramount importance, and I'm grateful for this partnership. Thank you for believing in my vision and for your unwavering support at every level to help bring this work to the masses. Jessica, Helen, Bridget, Francis, Ginia, Oghosa, and all the team. Thanks for the robust plan.

NOTES

Chapter 1 | WHAT DO YOU THINK OF WHEN YOU HEAR THE WORD *CHURCH*?

1. "Faith Among Black Americans," Pew Research Center, February 16, 2021, www.pewresearch.org/religion/2021/02/16/faith-among -black-americans.
2. "Why Black Churches Are Doing a $11.5 Billion Disservice to the Black Community," Urban Intellectuals, April 21, 2016, urbanintellectuals.com/black-churches-disservice-black-community.
3. Timothy Keller, *Counterfeit Gods: The Empty Promises of Money, Sex, and Power, and the Only Hope That Matters* (Penguin, 2009), 98–99.
4. Brandon Washington, *A Burning House: Redeeming American Evangelicalism by Examining Its History, Mission, and Message* (Zondervan, 2023), 23–24.
5. Washington, *Burning House*, 124–25.
6. Clinton E. Arnold, ed., *Zondervan Illustrated Bible Backgrounds Commentary: John, Acts* (Zondervan, 2002), 2:145.
7. Craig S. Keener, *The IVP Bible Background Commentary: New Testament*, 2nd ed. (IVP Academic, 2014), 293.
8. David Kinnaman, quoted in Kate Shellnutt, "Why Church Can't Be the Same After the Pandemic," *Christianity Today*, July/August 2021, www

.christianitytoday.com/2021/06/church-after-covid-pandemic
-trauma-tension-healing-together.

9. Kinnaman, quoted in Shellnutt, "Why Church Can't Be the Same."

10. Shellnutt, "Why Church Can't Be the Same."

11. Kinnaman, quoted in Shellnutt, "Why Church Can't Be the Same."

12. Robert H. Stein, "Differences in the Gospels," in CSB Study Bible: Notes, ed. Edwin A. Blum and Trevin Wax (Holman, 2017), 1513–14.

13. Clinton E. Arnold, ed., Zondervan Illustrated Bible Backgrounds Commentary: Matthew, Mark, Luke (Zondervan, 2002), 1:102.

14. Craig S. Keener, The IVP Bible Background Commentary: New Testament (InterVarsity, 1993), Matthew 16:14.

15. Paul Enns, The Moody Handbook of Theology, rev. ed. (Moody, 2014), 114.

16. Michael Heiser, The Unseen Realm: Recovering the Supernatural Worldview of the Bible (Lexham, 2015), 283–84.

17. Ken Carter and Audrey Warren, "Networks and Third Places Are Today's Mission Field," Lewis Center for Church Leadership, August 9, 2017, www.churchleadership.com/leading-ideas/networks-third -places-todays-mission-field.

Chapter 2 | BRAND AMBASSADORS

1. "Branding," Entrepreneur, www.entrepreneur.com/encyclopedia /branding.

2. Ross Kimbarovsky, "Rebranding: What It Is, Why It's Important, Strategies, and Examples [2024]," Crowdspring, updated February 26, 2024, www.crowdspring.com/blog/how-to-rebrand.

3. "Brand Ambassador: Meaning, Profiles and Examples," Influencity, October 25, 2024, https://influencity.com/blog/en/brand -ambassador-meaning-profiles-and-examples.

4. Melissa Sonntag, "Brand Ambassador: Definition, Job Description, Salary, and More," Repsly, www.repsly.com/blog/field-team -management/brand-ambassador-job-definition-description-salary.

5. Craig S. Keener, The IVP Bible Background Commentary: New Testament, 2nd ed. (IVP Academic, 2014), 508.

6. Paul Enns, The Moody Handbook of Theology, rev. ed. (Moody, 2014), 210.

7. Mark R. Gornik, To Live in Peace: Biblical Faith and the Changing Inner City (Eerdmans, 2002), 10.

8. C. Eric Lincoln and Lawrence H. Mamiya, *The Black Church in the African American Experience* (Duke University Press, 1990), 383.

9. John J. Dilulio Jr., "Living Faith: The Black Church Outreach Tradition," Manhattan Institute, March 1, 1998, manhattan.institute /article/living-faith-the-black-church-outreach-tradition.

10. Dilulio, "Living Faith."

Chapter 3 | REBRANDING CHURCH LEADERSHIP

1. Celina Tebor and Eric Levenson, "Brooklyn Pastor Who Was Robbed While Preaching Charged with Wire Fraud and Lying to FBI in Unrelated Case," CNN, December 20, 2022, www.cnn.com/2022/ 12/19/us/brooklyn-pastor-lamor-whitehead-fraud/index.html.

2. George W. Knight III, *The Pastoral Epistles: A Commentary on the Greek Text* (Eerdmans, 1992), 155–56.

3. Henry Blackaby and Richard Blackaby, *Spiritual Leadership: Moving People on to God's Agenda* (Broadman & Holman, 2011), 19, 75.

4. Timothy Friberg et al., *Analytical Lexicon of the Greek New Testament*, Baker's Greek New Testament Library (Baker Books, 2000), 164.

5. Craig S. Keener, *The IVP Bible Background Commentary: New Testament*, 2nd ed. (IVP Academic, 2014), 517.

6. Kendell H. Easley, "2 Corinthians," in *CSB Study Bible: Notes*, ed. Edwin A. Blum and Trevin Wax (Holman, 2017), 1851.

7. John H. Walton, *Zondervan Illustrated Bible Backgrounds Commentary: Isaiah, Jeremiah, Lamentations, Ezekiel, Daniel* (Zondervan, 2009), 4:478.

8. Jerome Gay, *Church Hurt: Holding the Church Accountable and Helping Hurt People Heal* (Renown, 2023), 12.

9. R. Laird Harris et al., eds., *Theological Wordbook of the Old Testament* (Moody, 1999), 366.

10. John H. Walton, *Zondervan Illustrated Bible Backgrounds Commentary: The Minor Prophets, Job, Psalms, Proverbs, Ecclesiastes, Song of Songs* (Zondervan, 2009), 5:340.

Chapter 4 | REBRANDING DISCIPLESHIP

1. A. W. Tozer, *Discipleship: What It Truly Means to Be a Christian—Collected Insights from A. W. Tozer* (Moody, 2018), 2.

2. Leon Morris, *The Gospel According to John*, rev. ed., The New International Commentary on the New Testament (Eerdmans, 1995), 137.

3. *Mishnah*, a codification of Jewish rabbinic oral tradition collected c. A.D. 200–220; *The NET Bible: Second Edition* (Biblical Studies Press, 2019), 1066.

4. *Vocabulary.com Dictionary*, "relativism," www.vocabulary.com/dictionary/relativism.

5. Robert Hampshire, "Should the Church Be Seeker Sensitive?," Christianity.com, December 22, 2020, www.christianity.com/church/should-the-church-be-seeker-sensitive.html.

6. "Signs of Spiritual Abuse," WebMD, www.webmd.com/mental-health/signs-spiritual-abuse.

7. "The State of Theology," thestateoftheology.com.

8. Craig S. Keener, *The IVP Bible Background Commentary: New Testament*, 2nd ed. (IVP Academic, 2014), 694.

9. "The word translated as 'basic principles' (*stoicheia*) could indicate basic principles, elementary truths, rudimentary elements (such as letters in an alphabet), the material elements of the world, or even elemental spirits believed to govern the world." Dana M. Harris, "Hebrews," in *The Baker Illustrated Bible Background Commentary*, ed. J. Scott Duvall and J. Daniel Hays (Baker Books, 2020), 1235.

10. J. I. Packer, *Knowing God* (IVP, 2023); Jen Wilkin and J. T. English, *You Are a Theologian: An Invitation to Know and Love God Well* (B&H Books, 2023).

11. Paul Enns, *The Moody Handbook of Theology*, rev. ed. (Moody, 2014); Wayne Grudem, *Systematic Theology*, 2nd ed. (Zondervan, 2020); Charles C. Ryrie, *Basic Theology: A Popular Systematic Guide to Understanding Biblical Truth* (Moody, 1999).

12. John Mark Comer, *Practicing the Way: Be with Jesus. Become like him. Do as he did.* (WaterBrook, 2024), 86.

13. Donald S. Whitney, *Spiritual Disciplines for the Christian Life* (NavPress, 2014), 4.

14. Whitney, *Spiritual Disciplines*, 5.

15. Eric Mason, *Unleashed: Being Conformed to the Image of Christ* (B&H Books, 2015).

16. Dietrich Bonhoeffer, *The Cost of Discipleship* (Touchstone, 1995), 89–90.

Chapter 5 | REBRANDING PREACHING AND TEACHING

1. George H. Guthrie, "2 Corinthians," in *The Baker Illustrated Bible Background Commentary*, ed. J. Scott Duvall and J. Daniel Hays (Baker Books, 2020), 1144.

2. Craig S. Keener, *The IVP Bible Background Commentary: New Testament*, 2nd ed. (IVP Academic: 2014), 516.

3. BibleTruthChannel (@bibletruthchannel), "The Greatest Threat to the Church," TikTok video, April 13, 2024, www.tiktok.com /@bibletruthchannel/video/7357383800613080326.

4. Haddon W. Robinson, *Biblical Preaching: The Development and Delivery of Expository Messages* (Baker Academic, 2014), 5.

5. David Helm, *Expositional Preaching: How We Speak God's Word Today* (Crossway, 2014), 13.

6. Hope Bolinger, "What Are Exegesis and Eisegesis? 2 Ways to Read the Bible," Christianity.com, February 25, 2022, www.christianity.com /wiki/christian-terms/what-are-exegesis-and-eisegesis.html.

7. Clinton E. Arnold, ed., *Zondervan Illustrated Bible Backgrounds Commentary: Romans to Philemon* (Zondervan, 2002), 3:492.

8. Keener, *IVP Bible Background Commentary*, 2 Timothy 4:4–5.

9. D. Edmond Hiebert, *Second Timothy*, Everyman's Bible Commentary (Moody, 1959), 107; see also the discussion in *The Vocabulary of the Greek Testament*, ed. J. H. Moulton and G. Milligan (1930 ed.). The verb also appears in 1 Timothy 1:6; 5:15; 6:20.

10. Thomas D. Lea and Hayne P. Griffin Jr., *1, 2 Timothy, Titus*, The New American Commentary (B&H Publishing, 1992), 34:244–45.

11. Charles C. Ryrie, *Basic Theology: A Popular Systematic Guide to Understanding Biblical Truth* (Moody, 1999), 125.

12. Grant R. Osborne, *The Hermeneutical Spiral: A Comprehensive Introduction to Biblical Interpretation* (IVP Academic, 2006), 21–22.

13. "False Teachers Have This in Common!," Smart Christians Life, YouTube video, May 20, 2024, youtu.be/SztY3s3fD8k?si=ogzadJ5CNtWI_00q.

14. "Adam Was More Perfect Than Jesus," Joy105 com, YouTube video, April 29, 2024, youtu.be/3tjuMTjjZsU?si=FUGO-BVU9XdJdrWv.

15. "Does Pastor Steven Furtick Teach Little 'Gods' Doctrine? YES!," By The Book Ministries, YouTube video, October 22, 2021, youtu.be/3U tKr4k1920?si=FnxuPvtypYrS2prs.

16. Michael J. Vlach, *Dispensational Hermeneutics: Interpretation Principles That Guide Dispensationalism's Understanding of the Bible's Storyline* (Theological Studies Press, 2022), 25.

17. Vlach, *Dispensational Hermeneutics*, 30.

18. Vlach, *Dispensational Hermeneutics*, 26.

19. G. K. Beale, *The Book of Revelation*, The New International Greek Testament Commentary (Eerdmans, 1999), 209–10.

20. "Crucifixion of Yehohanan. Study of the wounds on Yehohanan's skeleton enabled osteologists to reconstruct his position on the cross. His arms were nailed above the wrists to the crossbeam. His legs were bent and twisted to one side, and a small sedile, or seat, supported only his left buttock. Courtesy *Israel Exploration Journal* Vol. 20, Numbers 1–2 (1970)." "A Tomb in Jerusalem Reveals the History of Crucifixion and Roman Crucifixion Methods," Biblical Archaeology Society, August 6, 2024, www.biblicalarchaeology.org/daily/biblical-topics /crucifixion/a-tomb-in-jerusalem-reveals-the-history-of-crucifixion -and-roman-crucifixion-methods.

21. Sidney Greidanus, *Preaching Christ from the Old Testament: A Contemporary Hermeneutical Method* (Eerdmans, 1999), 29.

Chapter 6 | REBRANDING PURPOSE AND DREAMING

1. Eric Mason, ed., *Urban Apologetics: Cults and Cultural Ideologies: Biblical and Theological Challenges Facing Christians* (Zondervan, 2023), 225.

2. Mason, *Urban Apologetics*, 228–29.

3. R. Douglas Geivett and Holly Pivec, *A New Apostolic Reformation?: A Biblical Response to a Worldwide Movement* (Lexham, 2014), 14.

4. Geivett and Pivec, *New Apostolic Reformation?*, 120.

5. Judy Franklin and Ellyn Davis, *The Physics of Heaven* (Double Portion, 2012).

6. Christopher Berg, *The New Age Trojan Horse: What Christians Should Know About Yoga and the Enneagram* (Beyond, 2021), 33.

7. Andrew Strom, *Why I Left the Prophetic Movement*, rev. ed. (Revival School, 2012), Kindle.

8. Strom, *Why I Left the Prophetic Movement*, Kindle.

9. There are dozens of examples in the Bible, but here are few: Jeremiah 1:4; 13:8; Ezekiel 33:23; Zechariah 7:1.

10. "What Is the Word of Faith Movement? Is It Biblical?," Compelling Truth, www.compellingtruth.org/word-faith.html.

11. John Eckhardt, *Deliverance and Spiritual Warfare Manual: A Comprehensive Guide to Living Free* (Charisma, 2014), 202.

12. Matt Slick, "What Is Dominion Theology?," Christian Apologetics and Research Ministry (CARM), May 5, 2022, carm.org/carm/what-is -dominion-theology.

13. Rick Warren, *The Purpose Driven Life: What on Earth Am I Here For?* (Zondervan, 2002), 21.

14. John H. Walton, *Zondervan Illustrated Bible Backgrounds Commentary: The Minor Prophets, Job, Psalms, Proverbs, Ecclesiastes, Song of Songs* (Zondervan, 2009), 5:489–90.

15. "Proverbs 19:21: New English Translation, footnote d," Bible Gateway, www.biblegateway.com/passage/?search=Proverbs%20 19%3A21&version=NET.

16. Jared C. Wilson, "5 Things the Seeker Movement Got Right," Gospel Coalition, October 20, 2016, www.thegospelcoalition.org/article /5-things-the-seeker-movement-got-right.

17. James Swanson, *A Dictionary of Biblical Languages with Semantic Domains: Hebrew (Old Testament)* (Logos Research Systems, 1997).

18. Swanson, *Dictionary of Biblical Languages.*

19. "Genesis 1:28: Footnotes," Bible Gateway, www.biblegateway.com /passage/?search=Genesis%201%3A28&version=NET.

20. *The NET Bible: First Edition* (Biblical Studies Press, 2005), 5.

21. John Piper, *Let the Nations Be Glad!: The Supremacy of God in Missions,* 2nd ed. (Baker Academic, 2022), 22–26. Please note that the Bible verses shown in this section are directly from the Bible versions noted and not directly quoted from Piper's book.

22. Craig S. Keener, *The IVP Bible Background Commentary: New Testament,* 2nd ed. (IVP Academic, 2014), 250.

23. Clinton E. Arnold, ed., *Zondervan Illustrated Bible Backgrounds Commentary: John, Acts* (Zondervan, 2002), 2:9–10.

Chapter 7 | REBRANDING THE CHURCH'S RELATIONSHIP WITH MEN

1. Sharif A. Bey, *The Blueprint: Moorish Musings on Noble Drew Ali's Divine Plan of the Age* (CreateSpace, 2012), back matter.

2. "Elijah Muhammad is not, of course, the founder of the Nation of Islam. That distinction belongs to Wali Fard Muhammad. His origin and activities prior to 1930 are of some dispute, though some connection with the Moorish Science Temple seems likely." Herbert Berg, "Elijah Muhammad: An African American Muslim Mufassir?," *Arabica* 45, no. 3 (1998): 320–46, www.jstor.org /stable/4057315.

3. Elijah Muhammad, *Message to the Blackman in America* (Secretarius MEMPS Publications, 1973), 18, 26.

4. C. Eric Lincoln and Lawrence H. Mamiya, *The Black Church in the African American Experience* (Duke University Press, 1990), 117.

5. "Study Examines 'Man in the House' Rules in the Voucher Program," National Low Income Housing Coalition, August 24, 2020, nlihc.org /resource/study-examines-man-house-rules-voucher-program.

6. Elijah Anderson, *Code of the Street: Decency, Violence, and the Moral Life of the Inner City* (W. W. Norton, 1999), 28.

7. "Should Celebrity Pastors Be Content Creators Instead?," Ruslan KD, YouTube video, January 20, 2022, www.youtube.com/watch?v= yZ5lI8i1ALA.

8. John H. Walton, *Zondervan Illustrated Bible Backgrounds Commentary: Joshua, Judges, Ruth, 1 & 2 Samuel* (Zondervan, 2009), 2:281.

9. Kelly D. Liebengood, "1–2 Peter," in *The Baker Illustrated Bible Background Commentary*, ed. J. Scott Duvall and J. Daniel Hays (Baker Books, 2020), 1276.

10. Joel Frank, quoted in LaKeisha Fleming, "How to Be More Emotionally Available in Your Relationships," Verywell Mind, January 24, 2024, www.verywellmind.com/emotional-availability-8431874.

11. Peter Scazzero, *Emotionally Healthy Spirituality: It's Impossible to Be Spiritually Mature While Remaining Emotionally Immature*, updated edition (Zondervan, 2017).

12. Kendra Cherry, "Compassion Fatigue: The Toll of Caring Too Much," Verywell Mind, April 16, 2023, www.verywellmind.com/compassion -fatigue-the-toll-of-caring-too-much-7377301.

13. Ricardo Hernandez, "33 The Series—Vision, Mission, and Values," Calvary Baptist Church, March 14, 2017, https://calvaryga.com /33-series-vision-mission-value/.

Chapter 8 | REBRANDING EVANGELISM AND MISSION

1. "*The Joe Budden Podcast* Episode 309 | No Cigarettes in the Church," Joe Budden TV, YouTube video, December 27, 2019, www .youtube.com/watch?v=pMS2C_gdPAI&ab_channel=JoeBuddenTV.

2. "Dr. Umar States the Black Church Benefits from Single Motherhood," *Hardly Initiated*, YouTube video, April 23, 2024, www.youtube.com /watch?v=0y972XZolFg.

3. "Dr. Umar's Issue with Black Religion," Joe Budden Clips, YouTube video, January 3, 2024, www.youtube.com/watch?v=txpAv8CLhhA.

4. W. E. B. Du Bois, *The Philadelphia Negro: A Social Study and History of Pennsylvania's Black American Population; Their Education, Environment and Work* (University of Pennsylvania Press, 1996), 61.

5. Du Bois, *Philadelphia Negro*, 61.

6. Du Bois, *Philadelphia Negro*, 226.

7. Johannes Verkuyl, quoted in Harvie Conn and Manuel Ortiz, *Urban Ministry: The Kingdom, the City, and the People of God* (IVP Academic, 2010), 421.

8. Tony Evans, *Our Witness to the World: Equipping the Church for Evangelism and Social Impact* (Moody, 2020), 11. We must not forget that the Great Commission is all about our being God's witnesses in the world, both as a collective church and as individual believers.

9. Thom Rainer, "Why Are Churches Dying?," Church Leaders, September 22, 2021, https://churchleaders.com/outreach-missions /outreach-missions-articles/308041-dying-churches-die.html.

10. Gene L. Green, *The Letters to the Thessalonians* (Eerdmans, 2002), 267.

11. Leon Morris, *The Gospel According to Matthew*, The Pillar New Testament Commentary (Eerdmans, 1992), 317.

12. Mark Water, *The Gospel of John Made Easy* (John Hunt, 2000), 24.

13. John M. Perkins, ed., *Restoring At-Risk Communities: Doing It Together and Doing It Right* (Baker Books, 1995), 21.

14. Tony Evans, *The Kingdom Agenda: Life Under God* (Moody, 1999), 12.

15. Mark R. Gornik, *To Live in Peace: Biblical Faith and the Changing Inner City* (Eerdmans, 2002), 122.

16. Harvie Conn and Manuel Ortiz, *Urban Ministry: The Kingdom, the City, and the People of God* (IVP Academic, 2010), 264.

17. James Spradley, quoted in Conn and Ortiz, *Urban Ministry*, 265.

18. Conn and Ortiz, *Urban Ministry*, 265.

19. Evans, *Kingdom Agenda*, 401.

20. Clinton E. Arnold, ed., *Zondervan Illustrated Bible Backgrounds Commentary: Romans to Philemon* (Zondervan, 2002), 3:398.

21. Arnold, *Zondervan Illustrated Bible Backgrounds*, 399.

22. Arnold, *Zondervan Illustrated Bible Backgrounds*, 399.

23. Darrell L. Guder, ed., *Missional Church: A Vision for the Sending of the Church in North America* (Eerdmans, 1998), 4.

24. Steve Sjogren, *101 Ways to Reach Your Community* (NavPress, 2001).

25. Sjogren, *101 Ways*, 27.

26. Sjogren, *101 Ways*, 61.

27. Doug Logan, *On the Block: Developing a Biblical Picture for Missional Engagement* (Moody, 2016), 171–72.

28. Sjogren, *101 Ways*, 92.

Chapter 9 | REBRANDING CHURCH MEMBERSHIP AND COMMUNITY

1. Mark Driscoll, covenant-community manual, unpublished.

2. Jonathan Leeman, *The Church and the Surprising Offense of God's Love: Reintroducing the Doctrines of Church Membership and Discipline* (Crossway, 2010), 217.

3. Bobby Jamieson, *Committing to One Another: Church Membership* (Crossway, 2012), 17–18.

4. The apostles were called "pillars" by Paul in Galatians 2:9. "Giving the right hand of fellowship" simply indicates that an agreement has been made. By shaking hands, we as leaders are agreeing to care for the souls of those joining our church, and by shaking our hands, those joining are committing to loving and serving the church.

5. Peter T. O'Brien, *The Letter to the Hebrews*, The Pillar New Testament Commentary (Eerdmans, 2010), 529.

6. This quote has been attributed to Scottish theologian Sinclair Ferguson.

7. Tim Chester and Steve Timmis, *Total Church: A Radical Reshaping Around Gospel and Community* (Crossway, 2008), 39.

Chapter 10 | REBRANDING JESUS CHRIST

1. *Zeitgeist*, directed by Peter Joseph, GMP LLC, 2007.
2. Timothy Freke and Peter Gandy, *The Jesus Mysteries: Was the "Original Jesus" a Pagan God?* (Harmony, 2001).
3. D. A. Carson, *The Gospel According to John* (Eerdmans, 1991), 556.
4. Sermons by Logos, "Philippians (Lesson 6)," s.v. "form (essence)," https://sermons.logos.com/sermons/402253-philippians-(lesson-6).
5. Paul Enns, *The Moody Handbook of Theology*, rev. ed. (Moody, 2014), 242.
6. Enns, *Moody Handbook*, 242.
7. Got Questions Ministries, *Got Questions? Bible Questions Answered* (Logos Bible Software, 2002–13).
8. Enns, *Moody Handbook*, 242–43.
9. John N. Oswalt, *The Book of Isaiah, Chapters 1–39*, The New International Commentary on the Old Testament (Eerdmans, 1986), 181.
10. Johannes Louw and Eugene Albert Nida, *Greek-English Lexicon of the New Testament: Based on Semantic Domains* (United Bible Societies, 1996), 339.
11. Clinton E. Arnold, ed., *Zondervan Illustrated Bible Backgrounds Commentary: Romans to Philemon* (Zondervan, 2002), 3:385.
12. Sermons by Logos, "Sermon Tone Analysis," https://sermons.logos.com/sermons/282863/tone.
13. Richard R. Melick Jr., *Philippians, Colossians, Philemon*, The New American Commentary (B&H Publishing, 1991), 32:256.
14. In a normative or ideological sense, relativism (whether cognitive, cultural, ethical, or religious) maintains that ultimately rationality norms or truth or criteria for assessing alternative perspectives all arise from particular contexts (sociocultural, historical, linguistic, conceptual) and thus are only applicable within those contexts.
15. A. Scott Moreau et al., eds., *Evangelical Dictionary of World Missions* (Baker Books, 2000), 817.
16. Jean M. Twenge and W. Keith Campbell, *The Narcissism Epidemic: Living in the Age of Entitlement* (Atria Books, 2009), 18.
17. Dietrich Bonhoeffer, *The Cost of Discipleship* (Touchstone, 1995), 89–90.

18. *The NET Bible: First Edition* (Biblical Studies Press, 2005), Romans 12:1, www.biblegateway.com/passage/?search=romans%2012%3A1&version =NET.

19. DJ Envy, Charlamagne tha God, and Jess Hilarious, "Tye Tribbet on Winning Grammy for Gospel, Battling Depression, Finding God Outside of Church + More," March 6, 2024, *The Breakfast Club*, video, 49:55, www.youtube.com/watch?v=SBRq4n-l5fw.

ABOUT THE AUTHOR

DR. ERIC MASON is married to Yvette, and they have four children. He is the founder and senior pastor of Epiphany Fellowship, as well as the founder and president of Thriving, host of *The Sanctuary Podcast*, and servant of the Remnant Movement. Dr. Mason holds a bachelor of science in psychology from Bowie State University, a master of theology from Dallas Theological Seminary, and a doctoral degree from Gordon-Conwell Theological Seminary. He is the author of numerous books, including *Woke Church*, *Manhood Restored*, and *Urban Apologetics*.

ABOUT THE TYPE

This book was set in Joanna, a typeface designed in 1930 by
Eric Gill (1882–1940). Named for his daughter, this face is
based on designs originally cut by the sixteenth-century type-
founder Robert Granjon (1513–89). With small, straight serifs
and its simple elegance, this face is notably distinguished and
versatile.

01 14